Contents

Classic miso broth

Preparation time: 45 minutes, servings: 12

Nutritional information: calories: 2579 kcal, carbohydrates: 44.5 g, fat: 231 g, protein: 74 g

Ingredients:

- 1 medium carrot (peeled and roughly chopped)
- ½ onion (peeled and roughly chopped)
- ½ apple (cored, peeled and roughly cut)
- 1 stalk of celery (roughly cut)
- 3 cloves of garlic (peeled)
- 120 ml coconut oil
- 2 tbsp sesame oil
- 340 g of ground meat
- 2 teaspoons of fresh ginger (sliced)
- 1 teaspoon siracha
- 2 tbsp soy sauce
- 1 teaspoon apple cider vinegar
- 1 teaspoon salt
- 1 tablespoon sesame or thaina
- 175 ml Shiro Miso (white miso, light and sweet)
- 175 ml Akamiso Miso (red miso, dark and salty)
- 475 ml of chicken or vegetable stock

Preparation:

1. Hook finely the carrot, onion, apple and celery stick.
2. Put coconut oil and 1 teaspoon sesame oil in a large pan over medium heat. Then the chopped vegetables and fruits are fried in the pan for about 10-12 minutes, until the onion is translucent and the apple is lightly browned. Then reduce the heat slightly.
3. Add the mead to the pan and wait about 8-10 minutes until the mead is no longer pink. Add the ginger, soy sauce, apple cider vinegar and salt and stir everything well.
4. Put the whole mixture in the food processor until the meat is finely ground. Alternatively, you can e.g. B. use a potato masher.
5. Add the sesame seeds and miso to the mixture and stir well. The consistency should be like a thick paste. This creates the miso foundation.
6. Bring the vegetable or chicken broth to a boil. Add 6 teaspoons of miso foundation.
7. Put the ready-made soup in two bowls (approx. 235 ml each) and add pasta and toppings as desired.

Simple dashi broth

Preparation time: 1 hour, servings: 4

Nutritional information: calories: 15 kcal, carbohydrates: 0.25 g, fat: 1 g, protein: 13 g

Ingredients:

- 10 g kombu
- 10 g bonito flakes
- 720 ml of water

Preparation:

1. Take a pot with min. 500 ml capacity and put the bonito flakes in one pot and kombu in the other.
2. Bring both pots to a boil and then let them simmer for 1 hour.
3. Finally, strain off the ingredients and add the two brews together.
4. Put 235 ml each in a soup bowl. Add pasta and toppings as desired.

Sapporo ramen

Preparation time: 30 minutes, servings: 4

Nutritional information **:** calories: 6865.5 kcal, carbohydrates: 817 g, fat: 230 g, protein: 366 g

Ingredients:

- 60 ml miso broth
- 1 liter of Tonkotsu broth
- 1 teaspoon coconut oil
- 12 pieces of Chashu (see page 122)
- 2 teaspoons unsalted butter
- 125 g of fresh corn
- 4 servings of ramen noodles
- 300 g of bean sprouts

Preparation:

1. Put two spoons of the miso broth in each soup bowl.
2. Heat the Tonkotsu broth in a large saucepan.
3. Sear the chashu in a pan for 1-2 minutes on each side.
4. While the broth continues to simmer, melt the butter in a pan and saute the corn for 2 minutes until it turns lightly brown.
5. Cook the ramen noodles.
6. Put the finished noodles in the soup bowl and add approx. 250 ml stock to each bowl. Divide the corn and bamboo shoots on the bowls and add 3 pieces of chashu to each bowl.

Hakata ramen

Preparation time: 30 minutes, servings: 4

Nutritional information: calories: 7187 kcal, carbohydrates: 803 g, fat: 242 g, protein: 417 g

Ingredients:

- 60 ml Shoyu broth
- 1 liter of Tonkotsu broth
- 1 teaspoon soy sauc e
- Pinch of salt
- 1 teaspoon coconut oil
- 12 pieces of Chashu (see page 122)
- 4 servings of ramen noodles
- 2 tsp fresh ginger (chopped)
- 120 g Mu-Err mushrooms (soak the dried mushrooms beforehand)

Preparation:

1. Put two spoons of the Shoyu broth in each soup bowl.
2. Heat the Tonkotsu broth in a large saucepan.
3. Sear the Chashu with the coconut oil in a pan for 1-2 minutes on each side.
4. Cook the ramen noodles.
5. Put the finished noodles in the soup bowl and add approx. 250 ml stock to each bowl. Divide the mu-err mushrooms and ginger on the bowls and add 3 pieces of chashu to each bowl.

Hakodate ramen

Preparation time: 30 minutes, servings: 4

Nutritional information: calories: 5477 kcal, carbohydrates: 745 g, fat: 141 g, protein: 298 g

Ingredients:

- 60 ml Shio broth
- 1 liter of chicken broth
- 1 teaspoon coconut oil
- 12 pieces of Chashu (see page 122)
- 4 servings of ramen noodles
- 1 spring onion (finely chopped)
- 150 g bean sprouts
- 150 g bamboo shoot s
- 1 sheet of nori (cut into strips approx. 7.5x1.5 cm)
- 2 soft-boiled eggs

Preparation:

1. Put two spoons of the Shio broth in each soup bowl.
2. Heat the chicken broth in a large saucepan.
3. Sear the Chashu with the coconut oil in a pan for 1-2 minutes on each side.
4. Cook the ramen noodles.
5. Put the finished noodles in the soup bowl and add about 250 ml of stock to each bowl. Divide the spring onions, bamboo shoots, bean sprouts and nori on the bowls and add 3 pieces of chashu and ½ soft-boiled egg to each bowl.

Asahikawa ramen

Preparation time: 30 minutes, servings: 4

Nutritional information: calories: 5409 kcal, carbohydrates: 738 g, fat: 137 g, protein: 296.4 g

Ingredients:

- 60 ml Shoyu broth
- 0.5 l Tonkotsu broth
- 0.5 l Assari broth
- 120 g Mu-Err mushrooms (soak the dried mushrooms beforehand)
- 1 teaspoon coconut oil
- 12 pieces of Chashu (see page 122)
- 4 servings of ramen noodles
- Bamboo shoots

Preparation:

1. Put two spoons of the Shoyu broth in each soup bowl.
2. Heat the Tonkotsu broth together with the Assari broth in a large saucepan.
3. Sear the Chashu with the coconut oil in a pan for 1-2 minutes on each side.
4. Cook the ramen noodles.
5. Put the finished noodles in the soup bowl and add approx. 250 ml stock to each bowl. Divide the Mu-Err mushrooms and the bamboo shoots on the bowls and add 3 pieces of Chashu to each bowl.

Kitakata ramen

Preparation time: 30 minutes, servings: 4

Nutritional information: calories: 5568 kcal, carbohydrates: 754 g, fat: 142 g, protein: 306 g

Ingredients:

- 60 ml Shio broth
- 0.5 l chicken stock
- 0.5 l Niboshi Dashi (see page 27)
- 1 teaspoon coconut oil
- 12 pieces of Chashu (see page 122)
- 4 servings of ramen noodles
- 1 spring onion (finely chopped)
- Bamboo shoots
- 2 soft-boiled eggs

Preparation:

1. Put two spoons of the Shoyu broth in each soup bowl.
2. In a large saucepan, heat the chicken broth with the Niboshi Dashi.
3. Sear the Chashu with the coconut oil in a pan for 1-2 minutes on each side.
4. Cook the ramen noodles.
5. Put the finished noodles in the soup bowl and add approx. 250 ml stock to each bowl. Divide the spring onions and bamboo shoots on the bowls and add 3 pieces of chashu and ½ soft-boiled egg to each bowl.

Kyoto ramen

Preparation time: 30 minutes, servings: 4

Nutritional information: calories: 5896 kcal, carbohydrates: 751 g, fat: 176 g, protein: 321 g

Ingredients:

- 60 ml Shoyu broth
- 1 liter of chicken and pork broth
- 1 teaspoon coconut oil
- 12 pieces of Chashu (see page 122)
- 4 servings of ramen noodles
- 4 teaspoons of butter
- 1 spring onion (finely chopped)
- Bamboo shoots

• 1 sheet of nori (cut into strips approx. 7.5x1.5 cm)

Preparation:

1. Put two spoons of the Shoyu broth in each soup bowl.
2. Heat the chicken and pork broth in a large saucepan.
3. Sear the Chashu with the coconut oil in a pan for 1-2 minutes on each side.
4. Cook the ramen noodles.
5. Put the finished noodles in the soup bowl and add approx. 250 ml stock to each bowl. Divide the spring onions, bamboo shoots and nori on the bowls and add 1 teaspoon butter and 3 pieces of chashu to each bowl.

Takayama ramen

Preparation time: 40 minutes, servings: 4

Nutritional information: calories: 5491 kcal, carbohydrates: 754 g, fat: 171.5 g, protein: 288 g

Ingredients:

• 250 ml Assari broth
• 750 ml chicken broth
• 1 teaspoon sesame oil
• 1 teaspoon fresh ginger (chopped)
• 2 cloves of garlic (chopped)
• 1 leek (only the white part, finely chopped)
• 4 teaspoons of soy sauce
• 2 teaspoons of sake
• 2 teaspoons of sugar
• 2 teaspoons of salt
• 1 teaspoon coconut oil
• 12 pieces of Chashu (see page 122)
• 4 servings of ramen noodles
• 4 teaspoons of butter
• 150 g bamboo shoots
• 1 sheet of nori (cut into strips approx. 7.5x1.5 cm)

Preparation:

1. Put the sesame oil in a large saucepan and fry the ginger and garlic for a minute. Add the chicken and assari broth and.
2. Wait for the broth to boil, then reduce the heat and add the leeks, sake, sugar and salt.
3. Sear the Chashu with the coconut oil in a pan for 1-2 minutes on each side.
4. Cook the ramen noodles.
5. Put the finished noodles in the soup bowl and add about 250 ml of stock to each bowl. Divide the bamboo shoots and nori on the bowls and add 3 pieces of chashu to each bowl.

Tokyo ramen

Preparation time: 30 minutes, servings: 4

Nutritional information: calories: 6651 kcal, carbohydrates: 851 g, fat: 182.4 g, protein: 342 g

Ingredients:

- 60 ml Shoyu broth
- 0.5 l chicken stock
- 0.5 l Assari broth
- 1 teaspoon coconut oil
- 12 pieces of Chashu (see page 122)
- 4 servings of ramen noodles
- 12 pieces of Narutomaki
- 150 g bean sprouts
- 1 spring onion (finely chopped)
- 2 soft-boiled eggs

Preparation:

1. Put two spoons of the Shoyu broth in each soup bowl.
2. Heat the chicken broth together with the assari in a large saucepan.
3. Sear the Chashu with the coconut oil in a pan for 1-2 minutes on each side.
4. Cook the ramen noodles.
5. Put the finished noodles in the soup bowl and add about 250 ml of stock to each bowl. Divide the spring onions and bean sprouts between the bowls and add 3 Narutomaki and ½ soft-boiled egg to each bowl.

Spicy tonkotsu ramen with grilled pork fillet, peanuts and coriander

Preparation time: 30 minutes + 4 hours, servings: 4

Nutritional information: calories: 2707 kcal, carbohydrates: 456 g, fat: 160.5 g, protein: 227 g

Ingredients:

For the fillet:
- 3 teaspoons of mirin (sweet rice wine)
- 2 teaspoons of soy sauce
- 2 teaspoons of sesame oil
- 1 tsp Shichimi Togarashi (7 spice powder)
- 1 clove of garlic (peeled and chopped)
- 450 g pork tenderloin

For the ramen:
- 60 ml Shoyu broth
- 1 liter of Tonkotsu broth
- 1 teaspoon soy sauce
- Pinch of salt
- 4 servings of ramen noodles
- 50 g peanuts (roasted and chopped)
- Coriander (chopped) as needed

Preparation:

1. Mix the mirin, soy sauce, sesame oil, shichimi togarashi and garlic in a bowl. Add the pork tenderloin, cover with the marinade and leave to marinate in the refrigerator for at least 4 hours.

2. Heat a pan and fry the fillet for 10-15 minutes. Turn it over and over until it's done.

3. Take the fillet out of the pan and let it rest for 10 minutes before slicing.

4. Put two spoons of the Shoyu broth in each soup bowl.

5. Heat the Tonkotsu broth in a large saucepan. Add the soy sauce and salt.

6. Cook the ramen noodles.

7. Put the finished noodles in the soup bowl and add about 250 ml Tonkotsu broth to each bowl. Add 3 pieces of pork fillet, 1 teaspoon of peanuts and 1 teaspoon of coriander to each bowl. Scatter a pinch of Shichimi Togarashi on top.

Shio Tonkotsu Ramen with Mayu

Preparation time: 30 minutes, servings: 4

Nutritional information: calories: 6923 kcal, carbohydrates: 849 g, fat: 243 g, protein: 354 g

Ingredients:

- 60 ml Shio broth
- 1 liter of Tonkotsu broth
- 1 teaspoon soy sauce
- Pinch of salt
- 12 pieces of Chashu (see page 122)
- 4 servings of ramen noodles
- 2 Ajitsuke Tamago (see page 124)
- 1 spring onion (sliced)
- 2 teaspoons of Mayu (see page 126)

Preparation:

1. Put two spoons of the Shio broth in each soup bowl.

2. Heat the Tonkotsu broth in a large saucepan. Add the soy sauce and salt.

3. Cook the ramen noodles.

4. Put the finished noodles in the soup bowl and add approx. 250 ml Tonkotsu broth to each bowl. Add 3 pieces of chashu, ½ ajitsuke tamago, spring onions and ½ teaspoon mayu to each bowl.

Spicy tonkotsu ramen with ginger pork

Preparation time: 30 minutes, servings: 4

Nutritional information: calories: 3000 kcal, carbohydrates: 240.4 g, fat: 134 g, protein: 224 g

Ingredients:

- 60 ml miso broth
- 1 liter of Tonkotsu broth

- 4 servings of ramen noodles
- 4 servings of ginger pork (see page 134)
- 2 soft-boiled eggs
- 1 spring onion (sliced)

Preparation:

1. Put two spoons of the miso broth in each soup bowl.
2. Heat the Tonkotsu broth in a large saucepan.
3. Cook the ramen noodles.
4. Put the finished noodles in the soup bowl and add about 250 ml Tonkotsu broth to each bowl. Add a serving of ginger pork, ½ soft-boiled egg and spring onions to each bowl.

Shoyu Tonkotsu Ramen with Shrimp and Mushrooms

Preparation time: 30 minutes, servings: 4

Nutritional information: calories: 3413 kcal, carbohydrates: 248 g, fat: 146 g, protein: 200 g

Ingredients:

- 60 ml Shoyu broth
- 1 liter of Tonkotsu broth
- 200 g of shrimp
- 200 g mushrooms
- 2 teaspoons of chili paste (e.g. Sambal Oelek)
- 2 teaspoons of sesame oil
- 4 servings of ramen noodles
- 2 soft-boiled eggs
- 1 spring onion (sliced)
- 300 g of bean sprouts

Preparation:

1. Put two spoons of the Shoyu broth in each soup bowl.
2. Heat the Tonkotsu broth in a large saucepan. When it cooks, reduce the heat and add shrimp and mushrooms. Wait 2-3 minutes and then add the chili paste and sesame oil.
3. Cook the ramen noodles.
4. Put the finished noodles in the soup bowl and add about 250 ml Tonkotsu broth to each bowl. Divide the shrimp and mushrooms on the bowls and add ½ soft-boiled egg, spring onions and a quarter of the bean sprouts to each bowl.

Tonkotsu ramen with mentaiko and shiitake mushrooms

Preparation time: 35 minutes, servings: 4

Nutritional information: calories: 2502 kcal, carbohydrates: 258 g, fat: 83 g, protein: 116 g

Ingredients:

- 60 ml Shio broth
- 1 liter of Tonkotsu broth
- 2 teaspoons of butter
- 240 g shiitake mushrooms (cut)
- 4 servings of ramen noodles
- 1 spring onion (sliced)
- 1 nori sheet (cut into approx. 7.5x1.5 cm strips)
- 60 g mentaiko (pollack roe)

Preparation:

1. Put two spoons of the Shio broth in each soup bowl.
2. Heat the Tonkotsu broth in a large saucepan.
3. Melt the butter in a large pan and add the shiitake mushrooms. Wait about 5 minutes until they turn soft and brown.
4. Cook the ramen noodles.
5. Put the finished noodles in the soup bowl and add about 250 ml Tonkotsu broth to each bowl. Divide the shiitake mushrooms into the bowls and add spring onions, a few strips of nori and mentaiko to each bowl.

Shoyu Ramen with Chicken Katsu and Broccoli

Preparation time: 45 minutes, servings: 4

Nutritional information: calories: 4863 kcal, carbohydrates: 105 g, fat: 354 g, protein: 309 g

Ingredients:

For the chicken katsu:
- 1 large chicken approx. 500 g (boneless and skin)
- 1 teaspoon salt
- 1 teaspoon pepper
- Oil for deep frying
- 1 large egg (beaten)
- 130 g breadcrumbs

For the ramen:
- 60 ml Shoyu broth
- 1 liter of chicken or vegetable stock
- 650 g broccoli leaves
- 4 servings of ramen noodles
- 1 spring onion
- 30 ml katsu sauc e

Preparation:

1. Cut the chicken breast in two horizontally. Divide both pieces again into 2 equal parts.
2. Heat a deep saucepan with about 8 cm of oil and wait until it is hot.
3. Put the egg and breadcrumbs in separate bowls. First, dip a piece of the chicken into the egg and cover it completely. After that, dip it in the breadcrumbs. Repeat for all the pieces of chicken.

4. Carefully add the breaded chicken to the hot oil and let it fry until golden brown. Take the chicken out of the oil and place on a paper towel to drain for 5 minutes. Then cut it into strips.

5. Put two spoons of the Shoyu broth in each soup bowl.

6. Heat the chicken or vegetable stock in a large saucepan and cook the broccoli leaves in it for about 4 minutes. Remove the broccoli leaves with a slotted spoon.

7. Cook the ramen noodles.

8. Put the finished noodles in the soup bowl and add approx. 250 ml stock to each bowl. Divide the broccoli between the bowls and add spring onions, 1 piece of the chicken and a little katsu sauce to each bowl.

Hakodate Shio Ramen with spicy chicken

Preparation time: 25 minutes, servings: 4

Nutritional information: calories: 2100 kcal, carbohydrates: 178 g, fat: 103 g, protein: 114 g

Ingredients:

- 450 g of chicke n
- ½ teaspoon salt
- 1 clove of garlic (minced)
- 1 teaspoon soy sauce
- 1 teaspoon of chili oil

- 60 ml Shio broth
- 750 ml vegetable or chicken broth
- 250 ml dashi broth
- 4 servings of ramen noodles
- 1 spring onion

Preparation:

1. Heat a pan and fry the chicken and salt in it. Add the garlic and cook for 1 minute. Add the soy sauce and remove the pan from the heat. Mix in the chili oil.

2. Put two spoons of the Shio broth in each soup bowl.

3. Heat the vegetable or chicken broth together with the dashi broth in a large saucepan.

4. Cook the ramen noodles.

5. Put the finished noodles in the soup bowl and add approx. 250 ml stock to each bowl. Divide the chicken between the bowls and add the spring onions.

Cheese ramen with chili oil, ajitsuke tamago and corn

Preparation time: 25 minutes, servings: 4

Nutritional information: calories: 3643 kcal, carbohydrates: 315 g, fat: 184 g, protein: 190 g

Ingredients:

- 60 ml Shoyu broth
- 1 liter of Tonkotsu broth
- 2 Ajitsuke Tamago (see page 124)
- 4 servings of ramen noodles
- 1 spring onion
- 125 g grated Gouda cheese
- 125 g of fresh corn
- 4 teaspoons of chili oil
- 2 teaspoons of butter

Preparation:

1. Put two spoons of the Shoyu broth in each soup bowl.
2. Heat the Tonkotsu broth in a large saucepan.
3. While the broth continues to simmer, melt the butter in a pan and saute the corn for 2 minutes until it turns lightly brown.
4. Cook the ramen noodles.
5. Put the finished noodles in the soup bowl and add about 250 ml Tonkotsu broth to each bowl. Divide the corn and Gouda on the skins and add spring onions, ½ Ajitsuke Tamago and a little chili oil to each bowl.

Shio ramen with duck, ajitsuke tamago and bean sprouts

Preparation time: 25 minutes, servings: 4

Nutritional information: calories: 2705 kcal, carbohydrates: 232 g, fat: 147 g, protein: 122 g

Ingredients:

- 2 pieces of duck breast
- 60 ml Shio broth
- 1 liter of chicken or vegetable stock
- 2 Ajitsuke Tamago (see page 124)
- 4 servings of ramen noodles
- 1 spring onion (finely chopped)
- 300 g of bean sprouts

Preparation:

1. Salt and pepper the duck breast.
2. Heat a large pan and fry the duck breast (skin facing down) for 20-25 minutes until the skin is crispy and nicely brown. Turn the duck breast over and cook for another 5 minutes. Take the duck out of the pan and let it rest for 10 minutes. After that, cut them into slices.
3. Put two spoons of the Shio broth in each soup bowl.
4. Heat the chicken or vegetable stock in a large saucepan.
5. Cook the ramen noodles.

6. Put the finished noodles in the soup bowl and add approx. 250 ml stock to each bowl. Divide the duck and spring onions between the bowls and add ½ Ajitsuke Tamago to each bowl.

Miso-ginger ramen with spinach and salmon

Preparation time: 25 minutes, servings: 4

Nutritional information: calories: 2201 kcal, carbohydrates: 186 g, fat: 138 g, protein: 97 g

Ingredients:

- 1 teaspoon sesame oil
- 450 g of salmon
- Pinch of salt
- 60 ml miso broth
- 2 tsp fresh ginger (chopped)
- 1 liter of chicken or vegetable stock
- 4 servings of ramen noodles
- 150 g of fresh spinac h
- 1 spring onion

Preparation:

1. Heat a large pan, add the sesame oil, salt and pepper and fry the salmon for 4-6 minutes on each side, until the salmon is cooked through and lightly brown.
2. Put one part of the ginger and two spoons of the miso broth in each soup bowl.
3. Heat the chicken or vegetable broth in a large saucepan. When the broth boils, reduce the heat and add the spinach for a minute. Remove the spinach with a slotted spoon and set it aside.
4. Cook the ramen noodles.
5. Put the finished noodles in the soup bowl and add approx. 250 ml stock to each bowl. Divide the salmon, spinach, and spring onions among the skins.

Spicy miso ramen with Brussels sprouts, shiitake mushrooms and bacon

Preparation time: 55 minutes, servings: 4

Nutritional information: calories: 4022 kcal, carbohydrates: 272 g, fat: 243 g, protein: 169 g

Ingredients:

- 450 g Brussels sprouts (washed and halved)
- 2 teaspoons of olive oil
- ½ teaspoon salt
- ½ teaspoon pepper

- 60 ml miso broth
- 1 liter of Tonkotsu broth
- 4 servings of ramen noodles
- 240 grams of baco n
- 240 g fresh shiitake mushrooms
- 4 teaspoons of chili oil
- 1 spring onion

Preparation:

1. Preheat the oven to 220 ° C.
2. Mix the Brussels sprouts, olive oil, salt and pepper in a large baking pan and leave them in the oven for about 25 minutes until they are nice and brown.
3. With the Brussels sprouts in the oven, fry the bacon in a pan for about 7-9 minutes until crispy. Place the bacon on a paper towel to drain. Take a teaspoon of fat from the pan.
4. In the same pan, fry the shiitake mushrooms until they are soft and brown for about 5 minutes.
5. Put two spoons of the miso broth in each soup bowl.
6. Heat the Tonkotsu broth in a large saucepan.
7. Cook the ramen noodles.
8. Put the finished noodles in the soup bowl and add approx. 250 ml stock to each bowl. Divide the Brussels sprouts, chili oil and mushrooms into the bowls. Crumble the bacon over it.

Spicy Tantanmen Ramen

Preparation time: 1 hour, servings: 4

Nutritional information: calories: 2327 kcal, carbohydrates: 247 g, fat: 82 g, protein: 160g

Ingredients:

- 4 servings of ramen noodles
- 800 ml of chicken and pork broth
- 4 tbsp Japanese sesame paste (alternatively tahini)
- 4 tbsp chili oi l
- 4 servings of crispy, hot minced pork (see page 134)
- 2-3 baby pak choi
- 100 g bean sprouts
- 4 spring onions (finely chopped)
- 4 Ajitsuke Tamago (see page 124)
- 4 tbsp sesame seeds

Preparation:

1. Toast the sesame seeds and set them aside.
2. Heat the broth in a saucepan and let it simmer.
3. Preheat soup bowls.
4. Cut up the pak choi leaves and blanch them in a separate saucepan with boiling water for 30 seconds. You can cook the ramen noodles in the same water.

5. Put 1 tablespoon each of sesame paste and 1 tablespoon of chilli oil in a bowl and mix it with a little broth.

6. Cook the ramen noodles.

7. Add a portion of ramen noodles to each bowl as well as an ajitsuke tamago, pak choi and minced meat. Add about 250 ml of stock to each bowl. Sprinkle the soup with spring onions and sesame seeds.

Miso ramen with fish

Preparation time: 35 minutes, servings: 4

Nutritional information: calories: 2246 kcal, carbohydrates: 529 g, fat: 94 g, protein: 98g

Ingredients:

- 4 servings of ramen noodles
- 1 spring onion (finely chopped)
- 80 ml miso broth
- 1 liter of chicken or vegetable stoc k
- 3 carrots (peeled and cut into strips)
- 2 teaspoons of chopped ginger
- 2 cloves of garlic (peeled and chopped)
- 2 tbsp coconut oil
- 4 mushrooms (halved and sliced)
- 200 g fish fillets
- 2 tbsp soy sauce
- 1 tbsp mirin
- 2 tbsp sesame oil
- 4 tbsp sesame seeds

Preparation:

1. Toast the sesame seeds and set them aside.

2. Heat the broth in a saucepan and let it simmer.

3. Preheat soup bowls.

4. Sear mushrooms in a saucepan. Reduce the heat and add the garlic and ginger.

5. Deglaze everything with the chicken or vegetable broth and add the miso broth. Let it simmer for about 5 minutes and then add the carrots, spring onions and fish. Let it simmer until the fish is done and add soy sauce, mirin and sesame oil.

6. Cook the ramen noodles.

7. Put a portion of ramen noodles in each bowl and add approx. 250 ml stock to each bowl. Sprinkle the soup with sesame seeds.

Shoyu ramen with fish and soft-boiled eggs

Preparation time: 35 minutes, servings: 4

Nutritional information: calories: 2698 kcal, carbohydrates: 536 g, fat: 124 g, protein: 141g

Ingredients:

- 4 servings of ramen noodles
- 1 spring onion (finely chopped)
- 60 ml Shoyu broth
- 1 liter of chicken or vegetable stock
- 3 carrots (peeled and cut into strips)
- 2 teaspoons of chopped ginger
- 2 cloves of garlic (peeled and chopped)
- 2 soft-boiled eggs
- 2 tbsp coconut oil
- 4 mushrooms (halved and sliced)
- 200 g fish fillets
- 2 tbsp soy sauce
- 1 tbsp mirin
- 2 tbsp sesame oil
- 4 tbsp sesame seeds

Preparation:

1. Toast the sesame seeds and set them aside.

2. Heat the broth in a saucepan and let it simmer.

3. Preheat soup bowls.

4. Sear mushrooms in a saucepan. Reduce the heat and add the garlic and ginger.

5. Deglaze everything with the chicken or vegetable broth and add the Shoyu broth. Let it simmer for about 5 minutes and then add the carrots, spring onions and fish. Let it simmer until the fish is done and add soy sauce, mirin and sesame oil.

6. Cook the ramen noodles.

7. Put a portion of ramen noodles in each bowl and add approx. 250 ml stock to each bowl. Sprinkle the soup with sesame seeds and add a ½ soft-boiled egg.

Spicy miso ramen with corn, spinach and ajitsuke tamago

Preparation time: 25 minutes, servings: 4

Nutritional information: calories: 1893 kcal, carbohydrates: 302 g, fat: 70.3 g, protein: 60.5 g

Ingredients:

- 60 ml miso soy broth (see page 25)
- 1 liter of dashi broth
- 150 g of fresh spinach
- 125 g of fresh corn
- 1 tbsp butter
- 4 servings of ramen noodles
- 2 Ajitsuke Tamago (see page 124)
- 1 spring onion (finely chopped)

Preparation:

1. Put two spoons of the miso broth in each soup bowl.

2. Heat the dashi broth in a large saucepan. When the broth boils, reduce the heat and add the spinach for a minute. Remove the spinach with a slotted spoon and set it aside.

3. While the broth continues to simmer, melt the butter in a pan and saute the corn for 2 minutes until it turns lightly brown.

4. Cook the ramen noodles.

5. Put the finished noodles in the soup bowl and add approx. 250 ml stock to each bowl. Divide the spinach, corn, and spring onions on the skins. Add ½ ajitsuke tamago.

Ramen with soft-boiled eggs and pak choi

Preparation time: 45 minutes, servings: 4

Nutritional information: calories: 2738 kcal, carbohydrates: 81.3 g, fat: 51.4 g, protein: 55 g

Ingredients:

- 4 servings of ramen noodles
- 1 liter of Assari broth
- 1 spring onion (finely chopped)
- 2 baby pak choi (halved)
- 2 soft-boiled eggs
- 6 carrots (peeled and roughly chopped)
- 2 tbsp miso paste
- 2 tbsp maple syrup
- 2 tbsp rice wine vinegar
- 1 tbsp soy sauce
- 2 tablespoons of vegetable oil
- 200 g smoked tofu
- 1 teaspoon cornstarch
- 1 dash of soy sauce
- 1 tbsp sesame oil

Preparation:

1. Heat the Assari broth in a large saucepan.
2. Preheat the oven to 220 ° C. Mix the miso paste, maple syrup, rice wine vinegar, sesame oil and soy sauce to make a sauce. Brush the cut surfaces of the pak choi and pour the rest over the carrots.
3. Cook the carrots in the oven for 30-40 minutes. For the last 10 minutes, place the pak choi with the cut surface facing up on the baking sheet.
4. Dice the tofu and mix it with the starch. Fry the tofu in vegetable oil in a pan for about 10 minutes until crispy. Finally, top it off with a dash of soy sauce.
5. Cook the ramen noodles.
6. Put the finished noodles in the soup bowl and add about 250 ml of stock to each bowl. Divide the spring onions, carrots, pak choi and tofu between the bowls and add a ½ soft-boiled egg to each.

Miso ramen with grilled eggplant , ginger and spinach

Preparation time: 30 minutes, servings: 4

Nutritional information: calories: 1405 kcal, carbohydrates: 243 g, fat: 34.2 g, protein: 40.8 g

Ingredients:

- 60 ml miso soy broth (see page 25)
- 1 l vegan dashi broth (see page 22)
- 150 g of fresh spinach
- 1 eggplant
- ½ teaspoon salt
- 4 servings of ramen noodles
- 2 Ajitsuke Tamago (see page 124)
- 1 spring onion (finely chopped)
- 2 tsp fresh ginger (chopped)

Preparation:

1. Prepare the grill and grill the eggplant close to the flame on all sides until the meat is soft and the skin is almost black, for about 10 minutes. Let the eggplant rest for a few minutes, then peel off the skin. Sprinkle them with salt.

2. Put two spoons of the miso broth in each soup bowl.

3. Heat the dashi broth in a large saucepan. When the broth boils, reduce the heat and add the spinach for a minute. Remove the spinach with a slotted spoon and set it aside.

4. Cook the ramen noodles.

5. Put the finished noodles in the soup bowl and add about 250 ml of stock to each bowl. Divide the spinach, eggplant, ginger and spring onions on the skins. Add ½ ajitsuke tamago.

Curry ramen with carrots, peas and soft-boiled eggs

Preparation time: 25 minutes, servings: 4

Nutritional information: calories: 1485 kcal, carbohydrates: 243 g, fat: 22.7 g, protein: 61 g

Ingredients:

- 2 cloves of garlic (peeled)
- 2 tsp fresh ginger (chopped)
- 1 teaspoon of curry powder
- 1 teaspoon brown sugar
- 1 teaspoon coriander
- 1 teaspoon turmeric
- ½ teaspoon salt
- 2 teaspoons of coconut oil
- 60 ml miso soy broth (see page 25)
- 1 l Assari broth (see page 26)
- 1 teaspoon soy sauce
- 2 carrots (peeled and roughly chopped)
- 200 g of peas
- 4 servings of ramen noodles
- 2 soft-boiled eggs
- 1 sheet of nori (approx. 8 cm in size)
- 4 radishes (thinly sliced)
- 1 spring onion (finely chopped)

Preparation:

1. Put the garlic, ginger, spring onion, brown sugar, curry powder, coriander, turmeric and salt in a food processor and make a paste.

2. Heat a saucepan and add a teaspoon of coconut oil and the curry paste. Boil it for a minute. Add the Assari broth and reduce the heat. Then add the soy sauce.

3. Heat a saucepan and add a teaspoon of coconut oil and the carrots. Fry the carrots until tender for about 5 minutes. Add the peas and wait another 2 minutes. Take the pot off the stove.

4. Put two spoons of the miso broth in each soup bowl.

5. Cook the ramen noodles.

6. Put the finished noodles in the soup bowl and add about 250 ml of stock to each bowl. Divide the vegetables, nori strips and the radishes into the bowls. Add ½ soft-boiled egg.

Shio Ramen with Menma, Ajitsuke Tamago and Tomorokoshi

Preparation time: 30 minutes, servings: 4

Nutritional information: calories: 3452 kcal, carbohydrates: 565 g, fat: 205 g, protein: 88.4 g

Ingredients:

- 60 ml Shio broth
- 1 liter of umami broth
- 4 servings of ramen noodles
- 2 Ajitsuke Tamago (see page 124)
- 1 spring onion (finely chopped)
- 4 servings of Menma (see page Menma (seasoned bamboo shoots) 120)
- 4 servings of tomorokoshi (see page 132)

Preparation:

1. Put two spoons of the Shio broth in each soup bowl.

2. Heat the umami broth in a large saucepan.

3. Cook the ramen noodles.

4. Put the finished noodles in the soup bowl and add approx. 250 ml umami broth to each bowl. Divide the spring onions, menma and tomorokoshi on the bowls and add ½ ajitsuke tamago to each bowl.

Cheese ramen with chili oil, soft-boiled eggs and corn

Preparation time: 25 minutes, servings: 4

Nutritional information **:** calories: 2298.3 kcal, carbohydrates: 254 g, fat: 230 g, protein: 91 g

Ingredients:

- 60 ml Shio broth
- 1 liter of umami broth
- 2 soft-boiled eggs
- 4 servings of ramen noodles

- 1 spring onion
- 125 g grated Gouda cheese
- 125 g of fresh corn
- 4 teaspoons of chili oil
- 2 teaspoons of butter

Preparation:

1. Put two spoons of the Shio broth in each soup bowl.
2. Heat the umami broth in a large saucepan.
3. While the broth continues to simmer, melt the butter in a pan and saute the corn for 2 minutes until it turns lightly brown.
4. Cook the ramen noodles.
5. Put the finished noodles in the soup bowl and add about 250 ml umami broth to each bowl. Divide the corn and Gouda cheese into the bowls and add spring onions, ½ soft-boiled egg and a little chili oil to each bowl.

Shio ramen with mayu and shiitake mushrooms

Preparation time: 30 minutes, servings: 4

Nutritional information: calories: 1580 kcal, carbohydrates: 250 g, fat: 54 g, protein: 39 g

Ingredients:

- 60 ml Shio broth
- 1 liter of Assari broth
- 4 servings of ramen noodles
- 2 Ajitsuke Tamago (see page 124)
- 1 spring onion (sliced)
- 2 teaspoons of Mayu (see page 126)
- 7 fresh shiitake mushrooms (cut into strips)

Preparation:

1. Put two spoons of the Shio broth in each soup bowl.
2. Heat the Assari broth in a large saucepan.
3. Cook the ramen noodles.
4. Put the finished noodles in the soup bowl and add approx. 250 ml Assari broth to each bowl. Add shiitake mushrooms, ½ Ajitsuke tamago, spring onions and ½ teaspoon mayu to each bowl.

Miso ramen with mentaiko and shiitake mushrooms

Preparation time: 35 minutes, servings: 4

Nutritional information: calories: 1235 kcal, carbohydrates: 191 g, fat: 6.2 g, protein: 54 g

Ingredients:

- 60 ml miso soy broth (see page 25)
- 1 liter of dashi broth
- 2 teaspoons of butter
- 240 g shiitake mushrooms (cut)
- 4 servings of ramen noodles
- 1 spring onion (sliced)
- 1 nori sheet (cut into approx. 7.5x1.5 cm strips)
- 60 g mentaiko (pollack roe)

Preparation:

1. Put two spoons of the miso broth in each soup bowl.
2. Heat the dashi broth in a large saucepan.
3. Melt the butter in a large pan and add the shiitake mushrooms. Wait about 5 minutes until they turn soft and brown.
4. Cook the ramen noodles.
5. Put the finished noodles in the soup bowl and add approx. 250 ml dashi stock to each bowl. Divide the shiitake mushrooms into the bowls and add spring onions, a few strips of nori and mentaiko to each bowl.

Shio ramen with tofu, ajitsuke tamago and bean sprouts

Preparation time: 25 minutes, servings: 4

Nutritional information: calories: 1975 kcal, carbohydrates: 289 g, fat: 194 g, protein: 73 g

Ingredients:

- 175 g tofu for soups (cut)
- 60 ml Shio broth
- 1 liter of vegetable stock
- 2 Ajitsuke Tamago (see page 124)
- 4 servings of ramen noodles
- 1 spring onion (finely chopped)
- 300 g of bean sprouts

Preparation:

1. Put two spoons of the Shio broth in each soup bowl.
2. Heat the vegetable stock in a large saucepan.
3. Cook the ramen noodles.
4. Put the finished noodles in the soup bowl and add approx. 250 ml stock to each bowl. Divide the tofu and spring onions between the bowls and add ½ Ajitsuke Tamago to each bowl.

Miso-ginger ramen with spinach and tofu

Preparation time: 25 minutes, servings: 4

Nutritional information: calories: 1547 kcal, carbohydrates: 236 g, fat: 169 g, protein: 59 g

Ingredients:

- 175 g tofu for soups (cut)
- 60 ml miso soy broth (see page 25)
- 2 tsp fresh ginger (chopped)
- 1 liter of vegetable stock
- 4 servings of ramen noodle s
- 150 g of fresh spinach
- 1 spring onion

Preparation:

1. Put one part of the ginger and two spoons of the miso broth in each soup bowl.
2. Heat the vegetable stock in a large saucepan. When the broth boils, reduce the heat and add the spinach for a minute. Remove the spinach with a slotted spoon and set it aside.
3. Cook the ramen noodles.
4. Put the finished noodles in the soup bowl and add approx. 250 ml stock to each bowl. Divide the tofu, spinach and spring onions on the skins.

Spicy miso ramen with Brussels sprouts, shiitake mushrooms and roasted nori

Preparation time: 55 minutes, servings: 4

Nutritional information: calories: 1384 kcal, carbohydrates: 277 g, fat: 32 g, protein: 60 g

Ingredients:

- 450 g Brussels sprouts (washed and halved)
- 2 teaspoons of olive oil
- ½ teaspoon salt
- ½ teaspoon pepper
- 60 ml miso soy broth (see page 25)
- 1 liter of Assari broth
- 4 servings of ramen noodles
- 4 servings of roasted nori (see page 123)
- 240 g fresh shiitake mushrooms
- 4 teaspoons of chili oi l
- 1 spring onion (finely chopped)

Preparation:

1. Preheat the oven to 220 ° C.
2. Mix the Brussels sprouts, olive oil, salt and pepper in a large baking pan and leave them in the oven for about 25 minutes until they are nice and brown.
3. In a pan, fry the shiitake mushrooms in olive oil until they are soft and brown, for about 5 minutes.

4. Put two spoons of the miso broth in each soup bowl.

5. Heat the Assari broth in a large saucepan.

6. Cook the ramen noodles.

7. Put the finished noodles in the soup bowl and add approx. 250 ml stock to each bowl. Divide the Brussels sprouts, chilli oil, spring onions and mushrooms on the bowls. Crumble the toasted nori over it.

Shio ramen with fried potatoes, ajitsuke tamago and garlic chips

Preparation time: 25 minutes, servings: 4

Nutritional information: calories: 1774 kcal, carbohydrates: 285 g, fat: 188 g, protein: 49 g

Ingredients:

- 60 ml Shio broth
- 1 liter of vegetable stock
- 2 Ajitsuke Tamago (see page 124)
- 4 servings of ramen noodles
- 1 spring onion (finely chopped)
- 4 servings of fried potatoes (see page 130)
- 4 servings of garlic chips (see page 128)

Preparation:

1. Put two spoons of the Shio broth in each soup bowl.

2. Heat the vegetable stock in a large saucepan.

3. Cook the ramen noodles.

4. Put the finished noodles in the soup bowl and add approx. 250 ml stock to each bowl. Divide the fried potatoes, garlic chips and spring onions between the bowls and add ½ Ajitsuke Tamago to each bowl.

Shio ramen with mu-err mushrooms and edamame

Preparation time: 30 minutes, servings: 4

Nutritional information: calories: 1905 kcal, carbohydrates: 259 g, fat: 171 g, protein: 97 g

Ingredients:

- 60 ml Shio broth
- 1 liter of vegetable stock
- 4 servings of ramen noodles
- 200 g edamame
- 2 teaspoons of coconut oil
- 2 tsp fresh ginger (chopped)
- 120 g Mu-Err mushrooms (soak the dried mushrooms beforehand)

Preparation:

1. Put two spoons of the Shio broth in each soup bowl.
2. Heat the vegetable stock in a large saucepan.
3. Heat the coconut oil in a pan and fry the frozen edamame for 2 minutes.
4. Cook the ramen noodles.
5. Put the finished noodles in the soup bowl and add about 250 ml of stock to each bowl. Divide the mu-err mushrooms, edamame and ginger on the bowls.

Shio ramen with shiitake mushrooms and bean sprouts

Preparation time: 30 minutes, servings: 4

Nutritional information: calories: 1330 kcal, carbohydrates: 212 g, fat: 22 g, protein: 54 g

Ingredients:

- 60 ml Shio broth
- 1 liter of Assari broth
- 4 servings of ramen noodles
- 2 soft-boiled eggs
- 1 spring onion (finely chopped)
- 300 g of bean sprouts
- 240 g fresh shiitake mushrooms

Preparation:

1. Put two spoons of the Shio broth in each soup bowl.
2. Heat the Assari broth in a large saucepan.
3. Cook the ramen noodles.
4. Put the finished noodles in the soup bowl and add approx. 250 ml Assari stock to each bowl. Divide the spring onions, bean sprouts and shiitake mushrooms on the bowls and add a ½ soft-boiled egg to each bowl.

Spicy miso ramen with grilled tofu, peanuts and coriander

Preparation time: 30 minutes + 4 hours, servings: 4

Nutritional information: calories: 2073 kcal, carbohydrates: 408 g, fat: 210 g, protein: 92 g

Ingredients:

For the tofu:
- 3 teaspoons of mirin (sweet rice wine)
- 2 teaspoons of soy sauce
- 2 teaspoons of sesame oil

- 1 tsp Shichimi Togarashi (7 spice powder)

For the ramen:
- 60 ml miso soy broth (see page 25)
- 1 liter of vegetable stock
- 1 teaspoon soy sauce
- Pinch of salt

- 1 clove of garlic (peeled and chopped)
- 450 g of tofu

- 4 servings of ramen noodles
- 50 g peanuts (roasted and chopped)
- Coriander (chopped) as needed

Preparation:

1. Mix the mirin, soy sauce, sesame oil, shichimi togarashi and garlic in a bowl. Then add the tofu, cover it with the marinade and let it marinate in the refrigerator for at least 4 hours.
2. Heat a pan and fry the tofu for 10-15 minutes.
3. Take the tofu out of the pan and let it sit for 10 minutes before slicing.
4. Put two spoons of the miso broth in each soup bowl.
5. Heat the vegetable stock in a large saucepan. Add the soy sauce and salt.
6. Cook the ramen noodles.
7. Put the finished noodles in the soup bowl and add about 250 ml of vegetable stock to each bowl. Add tofu, 1 teaspoon of peanuts and 1 teaspoon of coriander to each bowl. Scatter a pinch of Shichimi Togarashi on top.

Shio ramen with bamboo shoots, aji-moyashi and tomorokoshi

Preparation time: 30 minutes, servings: 4

Nutritional information: calories: 3406 kcal, carbohydrates: 529 g, fat: 234 g, protein: 100 g

Ingredients:

- 60 ml Shio broth
- 1 liter of umami broth
- 4 servings of ramen noodles
- 4 servings of Aji-Moyashi (see page 126)

- 1 spring onion (finely chopped)
- 150 g bamboo shoots
- 4 servings of tomorokoshi (see page 132)

Preparation:

1. Put two spoons of the Shio broth in each soup bowl.
2. Heat the umami broth in a large saucepan.
3. Cook the ramen noodles.
4. Put the finished noodles in the soup bowl and add about 250 ml umami broth to each bowl. Divide the spring onions, aji-moyashi, bamboo shoots and tomorokoshi into the bowls.

Miso-ginger ramen with Horenso Gomare

Preparation time: 25 minutes, servings: 4

Nutritional information: calories: 2340 kcal, carbohydrates: 234 g, fat: 217 g, protein: 91 g

Ingredients:

- 175 g tofu for soups (cut)
- 60 ml miso soy broth (see page 25)
- 2 tsp fresh ginger (chopped)
- 1 liter of vegetable stock
- 4 servings of ramen noodles
- 4 servings of Horenso Gomare (see page 132)
- 1 spring onion

Preparation:

1. Put one part of the ginger and two spoons of the miso broth in each soup bowl.
2. Heat the vegetable stock in a large saucepan.
3. Cook the ramen noodles.
4. Put the finished noodles in the soup bowl and add approx. 250 ml stock to each bowl. Divide the tofu, horenso gomare and spring onions on the skins.

Spicy ramen with ajitsuke tamago and shiitake mushrooms

Preparation time: 30 minutes, servings: 4

Nutritional information: calories: 2076 kcal, carbohydrates: 313 g, fat: 197 g, protein: 81 g

Ingredients:

- 4 servings of ramen noodles
- 1 liter of vegetable stoc k
- 1 spring onion (finely chopped)
- 7 fresh shiitake mushrooms (cut into strips)
- 2 Ajitsuke Tamago (see page 124)
- 1 sheet of nori (cut into strips approx. 7.5x1.5 cm)
- 175 g tofu for soups (cut)
- 100 g bean sprouts
- 3 cloves of garlic (peeled and chopped)
- 2 tbsp coconut oil
- ½ teaspoon chilli flakes
- 3 teaspoons of miso

Preparation:

1. Fry the garlic in coconut oil. Before it turns brown, add the miso and chilli flakes and pour the vegetable stock on top.

2. Cook the ramen noodles.

5. Put the finished noodles in the soup bowl and add about 250 ml of stock to each bowl. Divide the spring onions, bean sprouts, tofu, shiitake mushrooms and nori on the bowls and add ½ Ajitsuke Tamago to each bowl.

Shio ramen with spicy tofu

Preparation time: 25 minutes, servings: 4

Nutritional information: calories: 1796 kcal, carbohydrates: 240 g, fat: 185 g, protein: 81 g

Ingredients:

- 450 g of tofu
- ½ teaspoon salt
- 1 clove of garlic (minced)
- 1 teaspoon soy sauce
- 1 teaspoon of chili oi l
- 60 ml Shio broth
- 750 ml vegetable stock
- 250 ml vegan dashi broth (see page 22)
- 4 servings of ramen noodles
- 1 spring onion

Preparation:

1. Heat a pan and fry the tofu with the salt in it. Add the garlic and cook for 1 minute. Add the soy sauce and remove the pan from the heat. Mix in the chilli oil.

2. Put two spoons of the Shio broth in each soup bowl.

3. Heat the vegetable stock with the dashi stock in a large saucepan.

4. Cook the ramen noodles.

5. Put the finished noodles in the soup bowl and add approx. 250 ml stock to each bowl. Divide the tofu on the skins and add the spring onions.

Spicy Shio Ramen with cabbage and corn

Preparation time: 25 minutes, servings: 4

Nutritional information: calories: 1941 kcal, carbohydrates: 261 g, fat: 201 g, protein: 60 g

Ingredients:

- 1 clove of garlic (minced)
- 1 teaspoon of chili oil
- 1 teaspoon soy sauce
- 60 ml Shio broth
- 750 ml vegetable stock
- 250 ml vegan dashi broth (see page 22)
- 4 servings of ramen noodles
- 1 spring onio n
- 125 g of fresh corn
- 1 tbsp butter
- 125 g of cabbage
- 4 tbsp sesame seeds
- 2 soft-boiled eggs

Preparation:

1. Toast the sesame seeds and garlic and set aside.
2. Season the cabbage with chili oil and soy sauce and cook it.
3. Put two spoons of the Shio broth in each soup bowl.
4. Heat the vegetable stock with the dashi stock in a large saucepan.
5. While the broth continues to simmer, melt the butter in a pan and saute the corn for 2 minutes until it turns lightly brown.
6. Cook the ramen noodles.
7. Put the finished noodles in the soup bowl and add approx. 250 ml stock to each bowl. Divide the corn and cabbage between the bowls and add ½ soft-boiled egg, sesame seeds and spring onions each.

Shio ramen with cabbage and soft-boiled eggs

Preparation time: 25 minutes, servings: 4

Nutritional information: calories: 1922 kcal, carbohydrates: 260 g, fat: 200 g, protein: 59 g

Ingredients:

- 1 clove of garlic (minced)
- 1 teaspoon soy sauc e
- 60 ml Shio broth
- 750 ml vegetable stock
- 250 ml vegan dashi broth (see page 22)
- 4 servings of ramen noodles
- 1 spring onion
- 125 g of fresh corn
- 1 tbsp butter
- 125 g of cabbage
- 4 tbsp sesame seeds
- 2 soft-boiled eggs

Preparation:

1. Toast the sesame seeds and garlic and set aside.
2. Season the cabbage with soy sauce and cook it.
3. Put two spoons of the Shio broth in each soup bowl.
4. Heat the vegetable stock with the dashi stock in a large saucepan.
5. While the broth continues to simmer, melt the butter in a pan and saute the corn for 2 minutes until it turns lightly brown.
6. Cook the ramen noodles.
7. Put the finished noodles in the soup bowl and add approx. 250 ml stock to each bowl. Divide the corn and cabbage between the bowls and add ½ soft-boiled egg, sesame seeds and spring onions each.

Miso ramen with shiitake mushrooms and ajitsuke tamago

Preparation time: 55 minutes, servings: 4

Nutritional information **:** calories: 1400kcal, carbohydrates: 280g, fat: 22 g, protein: 60 g

Ingredients:

- 450 g Brussels sprouts (washed and halved)
- 2 teaspoons of olive oil
- ½ teaspoon salt
- ½ teaspoon pepper
- 60 ml miso soy broth (see page 25)
- 1 liter of Assari broth
- 4 servings of ramen noodles
- 4 servings of roasted nori (see page 123)
- 240 g fresh shiitake mushrooms
- 1 spring onion (finely chopped)
- 2 Ajitsuke Tamago (see page 124)

Preparation:

1. Preheat the oven to 220 ° C.
2. Mix the Brussels sprouts, olive oil, salt and pepper in a large baking pan and leave them in the oven for about 25 minutes until they are nice and brown.
3. In a pan, fry the shiitake mushrooms in olive oil until they are soft and brown, for about 5 minutes.
4. Put two spoons of the miso broth in each soup bowl.
5. Heat the Assari broth in a large saucepan.
6. Cook the ramen noodles.
7. Put the finished noodles in the soup bowl and add approx. 250 ml stock to each bowl. Divide the Brussels sprouts, spring onions and mushrooms on the bowls. Crumble the toasted nori over it and add ½ Ajitsuke Tamago to each.

Shiitake Shio Ramen with silk tofu and crispy spring onions

Preparation time: 35 minutes, servings: 4

Nutritional information: calories: 997 kcal, carbohydrates: 187 g, fat: 11.6 g, protein: 30.2 g

Ingredients:

- 3 teaspoons of coconut oil
- 110 g fresh shiitake mushrooms (cut)
- 1 clove of garlic (minced)
- Pinch of salt
- 1 spring onion (finely chopped)
- 60 ml Shio broth
- 1 l vegan dashi broth (see page 22)
- 4 servings of ramen noodles

• 110 g silken tofu

Preparation:

1. Put 1 teaspoon of coconut oil in a hot pan over medium heat. Fry the shiitake mushrooms, garlic and salt for about 5 minutes.
2. Mix the spring onions and remaining oil in a small bowl. Spread them on a plate and put it in the microwave. Start the microwave over and over again for 30 seconds until the spring onions turn golden brown.
3. Put two spoons of the Shio broth in each soup bowl.
4. Heat the vegan dashi broth in a large saucepan.
5. Cook the ramen noodles.
6. Put the finished noodles in the soup bowl and add about 250 ml of stock to each bowl. Divide the shiitake mushrooms, spring onions and silken tofu on the bowls.

Miso-ginger ramen with tofu and bean sprouts

Preparation time: 25 minutes, servings: 4

Nutritional information: calories: 1561 kcal, carbohydrates: 244 g, fat: 166 g, protein: 61 g

Ingredients:

- 175 g tofu for soups (cut)
- 60 ml miso soy broth (see page 25)
- 2 tsp fresh ginger (chopped)
- 1 liter of vegetable stock
- 4 servings of ramen noodles
- 150 g of fresh spinach
- 1 spring onion
- 100 g bean sprouts

Preparation:

1. Put one part of the ginger and two spoons of the miso broth in each soup bowl.
2. Heat the vegetable stock in a large saucepan. When the broth boils, reduce the heat and add the spinach for a minute. Remove the spinach with a slotted spoon and set it aside.
3. Cook the ramen noodles.
4. Put the finished noodles in the soup bowl and add approx. 250 ml stock to each bowl. Divide the tofu, bean sprouts, spinach and spring onions on the skins.

Creamy peanut sesame ramen with vegetables

Preparation time: 30 minutes, servings: 4

Nutritional information: calories: 2035 kcal, carbohydrates: 337 g, fat: 47 g, protein: 59 g

Ingredients:

- 4 servings of ramen noodles
- 200 g edamame
- 2 carrots (peeled and cut into thin strips)
- 3 tbsp peanut butter
- 80 ml soy sauce
- 200 ml of water
- 2 tbsp sesame oil
- 3 tablespoons of lemon juice
- 7 tbsp maple syrup
- 3 tbsp cornstarch
- 1 clove of garlic
- ½ teaspoon pepper
- Coconut oil for frying
- Sesame

Preparation:

1. Mix the water, soy sauce, cornstarch, maple syrup, sesame oil, lemon juice and peanut butter with a whisk to make a sauce. Squeeze the garlic clove and add it.
2. Heat the coconut oil in a pan and fry the frozen edamame for 2 minutes.
3. Cook the ramen noodles halfway through the cooking time.
4. Add the sauce and let it simmer over medium heat. Then add the ramen noodles and the carrot sticks to the pan. Stir everything well to distribute everything evenly.
5. Garnish the ramen with sesame seeds.

Ramen with pak coi and carrots

Preparation time: 45 minutes, servings: 4

Nutritional information: calories: 1535 kcal, carbohydrates: 282 g, fat: 20 g, protein: 45.2 g

Ingredients:

- 4 servings of ramen noodles
- 1 liter of Assari broth
- 1 spring onion (finely chopped)
- 2 baby pak choi (halved)
- 6 carrots (peeled and roughly chopped)
- 2 tbsp miso paste
- 2 tbsp maple syrup
- 2 tbsp rice wine vinegar
- 1 tbsp soy sauce
- 2 tablespoons of vegetable oil
- 200 g smoked tofu
- 1 teaspoon cornstarch
- 1 dash of soy sauce
- 1 tbsp sesame oil

Preparation:

1. Heat the Assari broth in a large saucepan.
2. Preheat the oven to 220 ° C. Mix the miso paste, maple syrup, rice wine vinegar, sesame oil and soy sauce to make a sauce. Brush the cut surfaces of the pak choi and pour the rest over the carrots.

3. Cook the carrots in the oven for 30-40 minutes. For the last 10 minutes, place the pak choi with the cut surface facing up on the baking sheet.

4. Dice the tofu and mix it with the starch. Fry the tofu in vegetable oil in a pan for about 10 minutes until crispy. Finally, top it off with a dash of soy sauce.

5. Cook the ramen noodles.

6. Put the finished noodles in the soup bowl and add about 250 ml of stock to each bowl. Divide the spring onions, carrots, pak choi and tofu on the bowls.

Spicy ramen with nori and shiitake mushrooms

Preparation time: 30 minutes, servings: 4

Nutritional information: calories: 1668 kcal, carbohydrates: 258 g, fat: 171 g, protein: 72 g

Ingredients:

- 4 servings of ramen noodles
- 1 liter of vegetable stock
- 1 spring onion (finely chopped)
- 7 fresh shiitake mushrooms (cut into strips)
- 1 sheet of nori (cut into strips approx. 7.5x1.5 cm)
- 175 g tofu for soups (cut)
- 100 g bean sprouts
- 3 cloves of garlic (peeled and chopped)
- 2 tbsp coconut oil
- ½ teaspoon chili flakes
- 3 teaspoons of miso

Preparation:

1. Fry the garlic in coconut oil. Before it turns brown, add the miso and chili flakes and pour the vegetable stock on top.

2. Cook the ramen noodles.

3. Put the finished noodles in the soup bowl and add about 250 ml of stock to each bowl. Divide the spring onions, bean sprouts, tofu, shiitake mushrooms and nori on the bowls.

Curry ramen with vegetables

Preparation time: 25 minutes, servings: 4

Nutritional information: calories: 1318 kcal, carbohydrates: 242 g, fat: 9.7 g, protein: 49.6 g

Ingredients:

- 2 cloves of garlic (peeled)
- 2 tsp fresh ginger (chopped)
- 1 teaspoon of curry powder
- 1 teaspoon brown sugar
- 1 teaspoon coriander
- 1 teaspoon turmeric
- ½ teaspoon salt
- 2 teaspoons of coconut oil

- 1 l Assari broth (see page 26)
- 1 teaspoon soy sauce
- 2 carrots (peeled and roughly chopped)
- 200 g of peas
- 4 servings of ramen noodles
- 1 sheet of nori (approx. 8 cm in size)
- 4 radishes (thinly sliced)
- 1 spring onion (finely chopped)

Preparation:

1. Put the garlic, ginger, spring onion, brown sugar, curry powder, coriander, turmeric and salt in a food processor and make a paste.
2. Heat a saucepan and add a teaspoon of coconut oil and the curry paste. Boil it for a minute. Add the Assari broth and reduce the heat. Then add the soy sauce.
3. Heat a saucepan and add a teaspoon of coconut oil and the carrots. Fry the carrots until tender for about 5 minutes. Add the peas and wait another 2 minutes. Take the pot off the stove.
4. Cook the ramen noodles.
5. Put the finished noodles in the soup bowl and add about 250 ml of stock to each bowl. Divide the vegetables, nori strips and the radishes into the bowls.

Assari ramen with mu-err mushrooms and edamame

Preparation time: 30 minutes, servings: 4

Nutritional information: calories: 1458 kcal, carbohydrates: 212 g, fat: 17 g, protein: 84 g

Ingredients:

- 1 liter of Assari broth
- 4 servings of ramen noodles
- 200 g edamame
- 2 teaspoons of coconut oil
- 2 tsp fresh ginger (chopped)
- 120 g Mu-Err mushrooms (soak the dried mushrooms beforehand)

Preparation:

1. Heat the vegetable stock in a large saucepan.
2. Heat the coconut oil in a pan and fry the frozen edamame for 2 minutes.
3. Cook the ramen noodles.
4. Put the finished noodles in the soup bowl and add about 250 ml of stock to each bowl. Divide the mu-err mushrooms, edamame and ginger on the bowls.

Spicy shiitake ramen with Brussels sprouts and roasted nori

Preparation time: 55 minutes, servings: 4

Nutritional information: calories: 1075 kcal, carbohydrates: 272 g, fat: 22 g, protein: 51 g

Ingredients:

- 450 g Brussels sprouts (washed and halved)
- 2 teaspoons of olive oil
- ½ teaspoon salt
- ½ teaspoon pepper
- 1 liter of Assari broth
- 4 servings of ramen noodles
- 4 servings of roasted nori (see page 123)
- 240 g fresh shiitake mushrooms
- 4 teaspoons of chili oil
- 1 spring onion (finely chopped)

Preparation:

1. Preheat the oven to 220 ° C.
2. Mix the Brussels sprouts, olive oil, salt and pepper in a large baking pan and leave them in the oven for about 25 minutes until they are nice and brown.
3. In a pan, fry the shiitake mushrooms in olive oil until they are soft and brown, for about 5 minutes.
4. Heat the Assari broth in a large saucepan.
5. Cook the ramen noodles.
6. Put the finished noodles in the soup bowl and add approx. 250 ml stock to each bowl. Divide the Brussels sprouts, chili oil, spring onions and mushrooms on the bowls. Crumble the toasted nori over it.

Shiitake ramen with Brussels sprouts

Preparation time: 45 minutes, servings: 4

Nutritional information **:** calories: 934 kcal, carbohydrates: 270.4 g, fat: 18 g, protein: 50.4 g

Ingredients:

- 450 g Brussels sprouts (washed and halved)
- 2 teaspoons of olive oil
- ½ teaspoon salt
- ½ teaspoon pepper
- 1 liter of Assari broth
- 4 servings of ramen noodles
- 240 g fresh shiitake mushrooms
- 1 spring onion (finely chopped)

Preparation:

1. Preheat the oven to 220 ° C.
2. Mix the Brussels sprouts, olive oil, salt and pepper in a large baking pan and leave them in the oven for about 25 minutes until they are nice and brown.
3. In a pan, fry the shiitake mushrooms in olive oil until they are soft and brown, for about 5 minutes.

4. Heat the Assari broth in a large saucepan.

5. Cook the ramen noodles.

6. Put the finished noodles in the soup bowl and add approx. 250 ml stock to each bowl. Divide the Brussels sprouts, spring onions and mushrooms on the bowls.

Lemongrass ramen with cashew nuts

Preparation time: 45 minutes, servings: 4

Nutritional information: calories: 2649 kcal, carbohydrates: 250 g, fat: 256 g, protein: 67.4 g

Ingredients:

- 2 red chilies
- 4 sticks of lemongras s
- 1 liter of vegetable stock
- 2 cans of coconut milk
- 4 servings of ramen noodles
- 2 tbsp mild curry powder
- 8 tbsp salted roasted cashew nuts
- 2 red onions
- 8 tbsp peanut oil
- 400 g baby spinach

Preparation:

1. Cook the ramen noodles.

2. Wash the chili peppers. Cut the lemongrass several times and put it in a large saucepan along with the stock, coconut milk, curry powder and the chili pepper. Bring it to a boil.

3. Chop roughly the cashew nuts. Peel the onion and cut it into strips. Heat the oil in a pan and fry the onion strips together with the cooked noodles and cashew nuts for about 4 minutes. Season with salt.

4. Sort, wash and spin the spinach.

5. Remove the lemongrass and chili pepper from the soup. Cook the spinach in the broth for about 2 minutes.

6. Pour the finished pasta mixture into the soup bowl and add approx. 250 ml of stock to each bowl.

Ramen with Matcha

Preparation time: 30 minutes, servings: 4

Nutritional information: calories: 1909 kcal, carbohydrates: 242 g, fat: 194 g, protein: 94 g

Ingredients:

- 120 g of pickled bamboo shoots
- 120 g of pickled yellow radis h
- 200 g smoked tofu
- 1 tbsp rapeseed oil
- 1 liter of vegetable stock
- 4 servings of ramen noodles
- 40 g of dried shiitake mushrooms

- 400 ml soy drink
- 4 tbsp miso paste

- 2 teaspoons of matcha powder
- 4 tbsp nori flakes

Preparation:

1. Drain the bamboo shoots and radish and cut everything into fine strips. Cut the tofu into 5 mm thick strips.
2. Heat the rapeseed oil in a pan and fry the tofu for about 5 minutes.
3. In a large saucepan, heat the vegetable stock with the mushrooms. Cook the whole thing for 10 minutes. Remove the mushrooms and add the soy drink.
4. Cook the ramen noodles.
5. Put a spoonful of the miso paste in each soup bowl. Add the matcha powder to the broth.
6. Put the finished noodles in the soup bowl and add approx. 250 ml stock to each bowl. Divide the sprouts, radish, tofu, and mushrooms on the bowls and sprinkle the soup with nori flakes.

Miso ramen with corn and fried potatoes

Preparation time: 25 minutes, servings: 4

Nutritional information: calories: 971 kcal, carbohydrates: 190 g, fat: 9 g, protein: 39 g

Ingredients:

- 60 ml miso soy broth (see page 25)
- 1 liter of dashi broth
- 125 g of fresh corn
- 4 servings of fried potatoes (see page 130)

- 1 tbsp coconut oil
- 4 servings of ramen noodles
- 1 spring onion (finely chopped)

Preparation:

1. Put two spoons of the miso broth in each soup bowl.
2. Heat the dashi broth in a large saucepan.
3. While the broth continues to simmer, add the coconut oil to a pan and fry the corn for 2 minutes until it turns lightly brown.
4. Cook the ramen noodles.
5. Put the finished noodles in the soup bowl and add about 250 ml of stock to each bowl. Divide the corn, potatoes, and spring onions on the skins.

Spicy miso ramen with fried potatoes

Preparation time: 25 minutes, servings: 4

Nutritional information: calories: 1072 kcal, carbohydrates: 192 g, fat: 19 g, protein: 40 g

Ingredients:

- 60 ml miso soy broth (see page 25)
- 1 liter of dashi broth
- 125 g of fresh corn
- 4 servings of fried potatoes (see page 130)
- 1 tbsp coconut oil
- 4 servings of ramen noodles
- 1 spring onion (finely chopped)
- 2 tbsp chilli oil

Preparation:

1. Put two spoons of the miso broth in each soup bowl.
2. Heat the dashi broth in a large saucepan.
3. While the broth continues to simmer, add the coconut oil to a pan and fry the corn for 2 minutes until it turns lightly brown.
4. Cook the ramen noodles.
5. Put the finished noodles in the soup bowl and add about 250 ml of stock to each bowl. Divide the corn, potatoes, and spring onions on the skins. Add half a spoonful of chili oil to each bowl.

Ramen with nori and shiitake mushrooms

Preparation time: 30 minutes, servings: 4

Nutritional information: calories: 1618 kcal, carbohydrates: 251 g, fat: 170 g, protein: 70 g

Ingredients:

- 4 servings of ramen noodles
- 1 liter of vegetable stock
- 1 spring onion (finely chopped)
- 7 fresh shiitake mushrooms (cut into strips)
- 1 sheet of nori (cut into strips approx. 7.5x1.5 cm)
- 175 g tofu for soups (cut)
- 100 g bean sprouts
- 3 cloves of garlic (peeled and chopped)
- 2 tbsp coconut oil
- 3 teaspoons of miso

Preparation:

1. Fry the garlic in coconut oil. Before it turns brown, add the miso and pour the vegetable stock on top.
2. Cook the ramen noodles.
3. Put the finished noodles in the soup bowl and add about 250 ml of stock to each bowl. Divide the spring onions, bean sprouts, tofu, shiitake mushrooms and nori on the bowls.

Shiitake Shio Ramen with tofu

Preparation time: 35 minutes, servings: 4

Nutritional information: calories: 1156 kcal, carbohydrates: 187 g, fat: 21.4 g, protein: 46 g

Ingredients:

- 3 teaspoons of coconut oil
- 110 g fresh shiitake mushrooms (cut)
- 1 clove of garlic (minced)
- Pinch of salt
- 1 spring onion (finely chopped)
- 60 ml Shio broth
- 1 l vegan dashi broth (see page 22)
- 4 servings of ramen noodles
- 110 g smoked tofu
- 100 g bamboo shoots

Preparation:

1. Put 1 teaspoon of coconut oil in a hot pan over medium heat. Fry the shiitake mushrooms, garlic, tofu and salt for about 5 minutes.
2. Mix the spring onions and remaining oil in a small bowl. Spread them on a plate and put it in the microwave. Start the microwave over and over again for 30 seconds until the spring onions turn golden brown.
3. Put two spoons of the Shio broth in each soup bowl.
4. Heat the vegan dashi broth in a large saucepan.
5. Cook the ramen noodles.
6. Put the finished noodles in the soup bowl and add about 250 ml of stock to each bowl. Divide the bamboo shoots, shiitake mushrooms, spring onions and smoked tofu on the bowls.

Ramen with tofu and pak choi

Preparation time: 30 minutes, servings: 4

Nutritional information: calories: 1699 kcal, carbohydrates: 223 g, fat: 54 g, protein: 83 g

Ingredients:

- 4 servings of ramen noodles
- 1 liter of Assari broth
- 1 spring onion (finely chopped)
- 2 baby pak choi (halved)
- 2 tbsp miso paste
- 2 tbsp maple syrup
- 2 tbsp rice wine vinegar
- 1 tbsp soy sauce
- 2 tablespoons of vegetable oil
- 200 g smoked tofu
- 1 teaspoon cornstarch
- 1 dash of soy sauce
- 1 tbsp sesame oil
- 2 soft-boiled eggs

Preparation:

1. Heat the Assari broth in a large saucepan.

2. Preheat the oven to 220 ° C. Mix the miso paste, maple syrup, rice wine vinegar, sesame oil and soy sauce to make a sauce. Brush the cut surfaces of the pak choi.

3. Cook the pak choi in the oven for 30-40 minutes with the cut surface facing up on a baking sheet.

4. Dice the tofu and mix it with the starch. Fry the tofu in vegetable oil in a pan for about 10 minutes until crispy. Finally, top it off with a dash of soy sauce.

5. Cook the ramen noodles.

6. Put the finished noodles in the soup bowl and add about 250 ml of stock to each bowl. Divide the spring onions, pak choi and tofu between the bowls and add a ½ soft-boiled egg to each.

Ramen with radishes and nori

Preparation time: 25 minutes, servings: 4

Nutritional information **:** calories: 1341 kcal, carbohydrates: 253.4 g, fat: 11 g, protein: 44 g

Ingredients:

- 2 cloves of garlic (peeled)
- 2 tsp fresh ginger (chopped)
- 1 teaspoon of curry powder
- 1 teaspoon brown sugar
- 1 teaspoon coriander
- 1 teaspoon turmeric
- ½ teaspoon salt
- 2 teaspoons of coconut oil
- 1 l Assari broth (see page 26)
- 1 teaspoon soy sauce
- 2 carrots (peeled and roughly chopped)
- 200 g corn
- 4 servings of ramen noodles
- 1 sheet of nori (approx. 8 cm in size)
- 4 radishes (thinly sliced)
- 1 spring onion (finely chopped)

Preparation:

1. Put the garlic, ginger, spring onion, brown sugar, curry powder, coriander, turmeric and salt in a food processor and make a paste.

2. Heat a saucepan and add a teaspoon of coconut oil and the curry paste. Boil it for a minute. Add the Assari broth and reduce the heat. Then add the soy sauce.

3. Heat a saucepan and add a teaspoon of coconut oil and the carrots. Fry the carrots until tender for about 5 minutes. Add the corn and wait another 2 minutes. Take the pot off the stove.

4. Cook the ramen noodles.

5. Put the finished noodles in the soup bowl and add about 250 ml of stock to each bowl. Divide the vegetables, nori strips and the radishes into the bowls.

Shiitake ramen with nori, tofu and bean sprouts

Preparation time: 30 minutes, servings: 4

Nutritional information: calories: 1659 kcal, carbohydrates: 258 g, fat: 171 g, protein: 71 g

Ingredients:

- 4 servings of ramen noodles
- 1 liter of vegetable stock
- 1 spring onion (finely chopped)
- 7 fresh shiitake mushrooms (cut into strips)
- 1 sheet of nori (cut into strips approx. 7.5x1.5 cm)
- 175 g tofu for soups (cut)
- 100 g bean sprouts
- 3 cloves of garlic (peeled and chopped)
- 2 tbsp coconut oil
- 3 teaspoons of miso

Preparation:

1. Fry the garlic in coconut oil. Before it turns brown, add the miso and pour the vegetable stock on top.
2. Cook the ramen noodles.
3. Put the finished noodles in the soup bowl and add about 250 ml of stock to each bowl. Divide the spring onions, bean sprouts, tofu, shiitake mushrooms and nori on the bowls.

Shio ramen with vegetables and aji moyashi

Preparation time: 25 minutes, servings: 4

Nutritional information: calories: 2021 kcal, carbohydrates: 281 g, fat: 192 g, protein: 73 g

Ingredients:

- 1 clove of garlic (minced)
- 1 teaspoon soy sauce
- 60 ml Shio broth
- 750 ml vegetable stock
- 250 ml vegan dashi broth (see page 22)
- 4 servings of ramen noodles
- 1 spring onion
- 125 g of fresh corn
- 1 tbsp coconut oil
- 125 g of cabbage
- 4 tbsp sesame seeds
- 4 servings of Aji-Moyashi (see page 126)

Preparation:

1. Toast the sesame seeds and garlic and set aside.
2. Season the cabbage with soy sauce and cook it.
3. Put two spoons of the Shio broth in each soup bowl.
4. Heat the vegetable stock with the dashi stock in a large saucepan.
5. While the broth continues to simmer, add the coconut oil to a pan and fry the corn for 2 minutes until it turns lightly brown.

6. Cook the ramen noodles.

7. Put the finished noodles in the soup bowl and add approx. 250 ml stock to each bowl. Divide the corn, cabbage and aji-moyashi into the bowls and add the sesame seeds and spring onions to each.

Assari ramen with mu-err mushrooms and cabbage

Preparation time: 30 minutes, servings: 4

Nutritional information: calories: 1360 kcal, carbohydrates: 211 g, fat: 10 g, protein: 67 g

Ingredients:

- 1 liter of Assari broth
- 4 servings of ramen noodles
- 125 g of fresh corn
- 1 tbsp coconut oil
- 125 g of cabbage
- 2 tsp fresh ginger (chopped)
- 1 teaspoon soy sauce
- 120 g Mu-Err mushrooms (soak the dried mushrooms beforehand)

Preparation:

1. Season the cabbage with soy sauce and cook it.

2. Heat the Assari broth in a large saucepan.

3. While the broth continues to simmer, add the coconut oil to a pan and fry the corn for 2 minutes until it turns lightly brown.

4. Cook the ramen noodles.

5. Put the finished noodles in the soup bowl and add about 250 ml of stock to each bowl. Divide the mu-err mushrooms, cabbage, corn and ginger on the bowls.

Ramen with bamboo shoots and tofu

Preparation time: 30 minutes, servings: 4

Nutritional information: calories: 1866 kcal, carbohydrates: 239 g, fat: 193 g, protein: 92 g

Ingredients:

- 120 g of pickled bamboo shoots
- 200 g smoked tofu
- 1 tbsp rapeseed oil
- 1 liter of vegetable stock
- 4 servings of ramen noodles
- 40 g of dried shiitake mushrooms
- 400 ml soy drink
- 4 tbsp miso paste
- 4 tbsp nori flakes

Preparation:

1. Let the bamboo shoots drain and cut everything into fine strips. Cut the tofu into 5 mm thick strips.
2. Heat the rapeseed oil in a pan and fry the tofu for about 5 minutes.
3. In a large saucepan, heat the vegetable stock with the mushrooms. Cook the whole thing for 10 minutes. Remove the mushrooms and add the soy drink.
4. Cook the ramen noodles.
5. Put a spoonful of miso paste in each soup bowl.
6. Put the finished noodles in the soup bowl and add approx. 250 ml stock to each bowl. Divide the sprouts, tofu and mushrooms on the bowls. Sprinkle the soup with nori flakes.

Shio ginger ramen with Horenso Gomare

Preparation time: 25 minutes, servings: 4

Nutritional information: calories: 2378 kcal, carbohydrates: 238 g, fat: 220 g, protein: 91 g

Ingredients:

- 175 g tofu for soups (cut)
- 60 ml Shio broth
- 2 tsp fresh ginger (chopped)
- 1 liter of vegetable stock
- 4 servings of ramen noodles
- 4 servings of Horenso Gomare (see page 132)
- 1 spring onion

Preparation:

1. Put one part of the ginger and two spoons of the Shio broth in each soup bowl.
2. Heat the vegetable stock in a large saucepan.
3. Cook the ramen noodles.
4. Put the finished noodles in the soup bowl and add approx. 250 ml stock to each bowl. Divide the tofu, horenso gomare and spring onions on the skins.

Spicy Shio Ramen with tofu and peanuts

Preparation time: 30 minutes + 4 hours, servings: 4

Nutritional information: calories: 2126 kcal, carbohydrates: 244 g, fat: 214 g, protein: 92 g

Ingredients:

For the tofu:
- 3 teaspoons of mirin (sweet rice wine)
- 2 teaspoons of soy sauce

- 2 teaspoons of sesame oil
- 1 tsp Shichimi Togarashi (7 spice powder)

For the ramen:
- 60 ml Shio broth
- 1 liter of vegetable stock
- 1 teaspoon soy sauce
- Pinch of salt

- 1 clove of garlic (peeled and chopped)
- 450 g of tofu

- 4 servings of ramen noodles
- 50 g peanuts (roasted and chopped)
- Coriander (chopped) as needed

Preparation:

1. Mix the mirin, soy sauce, sesame oil, shichimi togarashi and garlic in a bowl. Then add the tofu, cover it with the marinade and let it marinate in the refrigerator for at least 4 hours.
2. Heat a pan and fry the tofu for 10-15 minutes.
3. Take the tofu out of the pan and let it sit for 10 minutes before slicing.
4. Put two spoons of the Shio broth in each soup bowl.
5. Heat the vegetable stock in a large saucepan. Add the soy sauce and salt.
6. Cook the ramen noodles.
7. Put the finished noodles in the soup bowl and add about 250 ml of vegetable stock to each bowl. Add tofu, 1 teaspoon of peanuts and 1 teaspoon of coriander to each bowl. Scatter a pinch of Shichimi Togarashi on top.

Ohitashi (chilled spinach salad)

Preparation time: 20 minutes, servings: 4

Nutritional information: calories: 265 kcal, carbohydrates: 20 g, fat: 12 g, protein: 12 g

Ingredients:

- 400 g of fresh spinach
- 140 ml dashi broth

- 2 teaspoons of soy sauce
- 6 teaspoons of bonito flakes

Preparation:

1. Cook the spinach for about 2 minutes. Squeeze out as much water as you can and roughly cut it.
2. Put dashi and soy sauce in a medium bowl. Add the spinach, stir everything well and put it in the fridge for 15 minutes.
3. Mix everything well again, divide the spinach into four bowls and pour the bonito flakes on top.

Sunomono (cucumber salad)

Preparation time: 20 minutes, servings: 4

Nutritional information: calories: 296 kcal, carbohydrates: 40 g, fat: 10.5 g, protein: 7.5 g

Ingredients:
- 2 cucumbers (thinly sliced)
- 1 teaspoon salt
- 125 ml rice vinegar
- 2 tbsp soy sauce
- 1 tbsp mirin
- 1 tbsp sugar
- 100 g carrots (peeled and grated)
- 4 tbsp toasted sesame seeds

Preparation:
1. Put the sliced cucumber in a bowl and sprinkle the salt over it. Let it stand for 10 minutes.
2. In a small bowl, mix the rice vinegar, soy sauce, sugar and mirin together. Stir until the sugar dissolves.
3. Squeeze out the cucumber slices and place them in a salad bowl. Add the dressing and mix well. Let the salad in the refrigerator for at least an hour before serving.
4. Divide the salad into four bowls and add the grated carrots and toasted sesame seeds.

Salted edamame

Preparation time: 15 minutes, servings: 3

Nutritional information: calories: 596 kcal, carbohydrates: 63.4 g, fat: 18 g, protein: 56 g

Ingredients:
- 450 g edamame (frozen)
- 3 tbsp salt + more to sprinkle on
- 2 tsp Shichimi Togarashi (7 spice powder)
- 2 teaspoons of soy sauce
- 2 teaspoons of lemon juice

Preparation:
1. Put the salt and the edamame in a large saucepan of boiling water. Cook the edamame until they are soft and still light green.
2. Drain the edamame and place on a paper towel. Sprinkle salt on top
3. Let the edamame dry for 2 minutes and then pour shichimi togarashi, soy sauce and lemon juice over it.

Tsukemono (cabbage, carrot and cucumber pickles)

Preparation time: 45 minutes, servings: 4

Nutritional information: calories: 182 kcal, carbohydrates: 25.5 g, fat: 2.4 g, protein: 7.5 g

Ingredients:

- 1 small head of cabbage (pitted and roughly cut)
- 1 carrot (peeled and cut into sticks)
- ½ cucumber (thinly sliced)
- 2 tablespoons of salt
- 1 teaspoon lemon peel
- 1 teaspoon red pepper flakes

Preparation:

1. Put the vegetables in a large bowl and add salt, lemon zest and pepper flakes. Mix everything well.
2. Place plastic wrap on the bowl and find a plate that fits snugly in the bowl. Put the plate in the bowl and put something heavy on top. Leave it in the fridge overnight.
3. Pour everything into a colander and drain well.

Nasu Dengaku (grilled eggplant)

Preparation time: 45 minutes, servings: 4

Nutritional information: calories: 406.4 kcal, carbohydrates: 52 g, fat: 18 g, protein: 13.6 g

Ingredients:

- 2 eggplants
- 1 teaspoon of oil
- 2 tbsp sake
- 2 tbsp mirin
- 125 ml of white miso
- 2 tablespoons of sugar
- 2 tbsp sesame seeds
- 2 spring onions (finely chopped)

Preparation:

1. Preheat the oven to 190 ° C.
2. Cut the eggplant lengthways once. Cut an x-shaped pattern in the cut surfaces. Coat the cut surfaces with oil. Place the eggplant pieces on a baking sheet with baking paper and bake for about 20 to 30 minutes, until they turn lightly brown.
3. Meanwhile, mix the sake and mirin together and heat it in a small saucepan. Add the miso and stir well. Add the sugar and reduce the heat. After three minutes, take the pot off the stove.
4. When the eggplant is ready, take it out of the oven and put the oven on grill. Pour the sauce over the eggplant, place it in a baking dish, cut side up, and put it in the oven. Wait until the sauce starts to bubble and caramelize for about 1 minute.
5. Take the eggplant out of the oven and sprinkle with spring onions and sesame seeds.

Yasai Itame (stir-fry vegetables)

Preparation time: 40 minutes, servings: 4

Nutritional information **:** calories: 826.4 kcal, carbohydrates: 72.4 g, fat: 42.4 g, protein: 25.5 g

Ingredients:

- 3 tbsp soy sauce
- 1 tbsp sake
- 1 tbsp sugar
- 1 tbsp sesame oil
- ¼ tbsp red pepper flakes
- 110 g tofu (cut into pieces)
- 2 tablespoons of oil
- ½ onion (peeled and cut)
- 1 small cabbage (roughly cut)
- 1 carrot (finely chopped)
- 100 g broccoli
- 4 large fresh shiitake mushrooms (cut into small pieces)
- 1 red pepper (pitted and cut into small pieces)
- 2 spring onions (finely chopped)
- 2 cloves of garlic (peeled and chopped)
- 1 tbsp chopped ginger

Preparation:

1. Put the soy sauce, sake, sugar, sesame oil and paprika flakes in a bowl and stir everything together. Add the tofu and turn it in the sauce. Set it aside for 30 minutes and remove the tofu from the sauce.

2. Fry the tofu in a pan with 1 teaspoon of oil for about 2-3 minutes.

3. Put another 1 teaspoon of oil in the pan and turn it on the highest setting.

4. Fry the onions for about 3 minutes, then add the cabbage and carrots and wait another 3 minutes. Add the broccoli and the shiitake mushrooms and wait another 2 minutes. Add the bell pepper and green onions and wait another 3 minutes. Lastly, add the garlic and ginger and wait another minute.

5. Add the tofu to the vegetables and mix well.

Burokkori Goma-ae (broccoli with sesame dressing)

Preparation time: 12 minutes, servings: 4

Nutritional information: calories: 357 kcal, carbohydrates: 22 g, fat: 19 g, protein: 29 g

Ingredients:

- 400 g broccoli
- 3 tbsp toasted sesame seeds
- 2 tbsp soy sauce
- 1 tbsp dashi broth
- 1 teaspoon of white miso
- 1 teaspoon of sugar

Preparation:

1. Blanch the broccoli in a saucepan of boiling water for about 3 to 5 minutes. Let it drain well and set it aside.

2. Put the sesame seeds in a small bowl and mash them with the back of a teaspoon.

3. Mix the soy sauce and dashi in a large bowl. Add miso and stir well. Add the sesame seeds and sugar and mix well.

4. Add the cooled broccoli and mix well.

Tsuma (Japanese radish)

Preparation time: 10 minutes, servings: 4

Nutritional information: calories: 28 kcal, carbohydrates: 4 g, fat: 0.3 g, protein: 2.1 g

Ingredients:

- 1 Japanese radish (peeled and ends cut off)

Preparation:

1. Cut the Japanese radish into long strips (e.g. with a vegetable peeler or grater):
2. Soak the radish in cold water for 15 minutes.
3. Dry well before serving.

Shishito peppers

Preparation time: 20 minutes, servings: 4

Nutritional information: calories: 205 kcal, carbohydrates: 16.2 g, fat: 12 g, protein: 3.6 g

Ingredients:

- 225 g shishito peppers
- 1 tbsp oil
- 2 teaspoons of salt
- 1 tbsp lemon juice
- 1 tsp Shichimi Togarashi (7 spice powder)

Preparation:

1. Heat the oil in a pan.
2. When the pan is hot, add the peppers and reduce the heat.
3. Fry the peppers for 10 -12 minutes. Apply them regularly.
4. Take the finished peppers out of the pan and sprinkle salt, lemon juice and Shichimi Togarashi over them.

Hiyayakko (chilled tofu)

Preparation time: 10 minutes, servings: 4

Nutritional information: calories: 432 kcal, carbohydrates: 20 g, fat: 39 g, protein: 28 g

Ingredients:

- 680 g silken tofu (chilled and cut into 1.5 cm pieces)
- 4 tbsp soy sauce
- 1 teaspoon of chopped fresh ginger
- 2 spring onions (finely chopped)
- 1 tbsp bonito flakes

Preparation:

1. Divide the tofu into four bowls. Add a spoonful of soy sauce and ¼ of the ginger to each bowl.
2. Sprinkle with spring onions and bonito flakes.

Japanese rice

Preparation time: 25 minutes, servings: 8

Nutritional information: calories: 508.4 kcal, carbohydrates: 112 g, fat: 1.2 g, protein: 11 g

Ingredients:

- 400 g Japanese rice
- 1 liter of water

Preparation:

1. Put the rice in a medium saucepan and cover it with about 5 cm of water. Mix and squeeze the rice with your hands until the water turns milky.
2. Pour the water off and repeat 3 times until the water runs clear.
3. Put the rice and the water (1 l) in a saucepan and cook for about 20 minutes. Let the rice sit for 10 minutes before serving.

Cya-han (Fried Rice)

Preparation time: 20 minutes, servings: 8

Nutritional information: calories: 1311 kcal, carbohydrates: 212 g, fat: 34 g, protein: 37 g

Ingredients:

- 4 strips of bacon
- ¼ red onion (peeled and finely chopped)
- 1 tbsp sesame oil
- 745 g Japanese rice (see page 105)
- 2 eggs
- 1 tbsp soy sauce

Preparation:

1. Fry the bacon well in a pan. Then place it on a paper towel & keep the fat in the pan.
2. In the same pan, fry the onions until they turn brown and add the sesame oil.
3. Add the rice and stir everything well. The rice makes a popping sound and turns crispy.
4. Make a hole in the middle of the rice and add the two eggs. Whisk the egg.
5. Mix the egg with the rice. Add soy sauce. Finally, crumble up the bacon and mix it in.

Gohan (sweet pork)

Preparation time: 30 minutes, servings: 6

Nutritional information: calories: 2657 kcal, carbohydrates: 319 g, fat: 81.4 g, protein: 154 g

Ingredients:

- ½ onion (peeled and finely chopped)
- 1 carrot (peeled and finely chopped)
- 1 tbsp sesame oil
- 455 g pork
- 1 tbsp soy sauce
- 1 tbsp sugar
- 1 tbsp sake
- 1 teaspoon ginger
- 1.1 kg Japanese rice (see page 105)
- 3 spring onions (finely chopped)

Preparation:

1. Heat the sesame oil in a large pan. Add the onion and carrot and fry for about 10 minutes.
2. Add the pork and wait until the meat is cooked through. Reduce the heat.
3. Mix the soy sauce, sugar, sake, and ginger in a small bowl.
4. Pour the sauce over the meat and stir everything well.
5. Mix everything with a blender until it has a fine consistency.
6. Put the rice in a bowl and add the meat. Scatter green onions on top.

Potato salad

Preparation time: 35 minutes, servings: 6

Nutritional information: calories: 2151 kcal, carbohydrates: 107 g, fat: 169 g, protein: 40 g

Ingredients:

- 2 teaspoons of salt
- 3 medium potatoes (peeled and halved)
- 3 eggs
- 3 slices of pancetta (pork belly)
- 80 g red onions (peeled and finely chopped)
- ½ cucumber (halved and finely chopped)
- 3 pickles (finely chopped)
- 1 carrot (peeled and finely chopped)
- 3 apples (cut into bite-sized pieces)
- 40 g parmesan cheese
- 175 g mayonnaise
- 60 g pickled radish
- 3 teaspoons of mustard
- Pinch of pepper

Preparation:

1. Cook the potatoes together with a teaspoon of salt in a saucepan for about 25 minutes, until they can be easily cut with a knife.
2. While the potatoes are cooking, place the eggs in a saucepan of cold water so that they are completely covered. Bring the water to a boil, remove the saucepan from the stove, put the lid on the saucepan and wait 10 minutes.
3. Put the eggs in an ice bath for 3 minutes. Peel the eggs and cut them into bite-sized pieces. Place the eggs in a bowl large enough to hold the entire salad.

4.   Add the pancetta, red onion, cucumber, pickles, and the carrot to the bowl.

5.   Drain the potatoes and let them cool. Cut them into bite-sized pieces. Add the parmesan and the apples to the bowl.

6.   Add mayonnaise, radish, mustard, salt and pepper and stir everything well. Serve chilled.

Crispy teriyaki chicken wings

Preparation time: 1 hour, servings: approx. 40 chicken wings

Nutritional information: calories: 4110 kcal, carbohydrates: 299 g, fat: 223 g, protein: 225 g

Ingredients:

- 475 ml of oil for deep-frying
- 110 g of flour
- 235 ml of water
- 3 ice cubes
- 1.1 kg of chicken wings
- 200 g of sugar
- 235 ml soy sauce
- 2 tbsp ginger
- 60 ml of mirin

Preparation:

1.   Mix sugar, soy sauce, ginger and mirin into a sauce.

2.   Heat the oil in a large saucepan. The oil should cover at least 4 cm.

3.   Mix the water and flour into a batter. Add the ice cubes. Keep stirring while the ice cubes melt.

4.   Test whether the oil is hot by adding a drop of batter. If it sizzles right away, the oil is hot enough.

5.   Flip the chicken wings in the batter and then deep-fry them until brown and crispy.

6.   Dip the chicken wings in the sauce for 5 seconds.

7.   Place the chicken wings on a rack to cool. Make sure the chicken wings aren't touching, this will keep them crispy.

Cucumber and avocado salad with carrot and ginger dressing

Preparation time: 5 minutes, servings: 4

Nutritional information: calories: 1180 kcal, carbohydrates: 30.2 g, fat: 104 g, protein: 12.3 g

Ingredients:

- 2 small carrots (peeled)
- 1 tbsp spring onions (finely chopped)
- 2 teaspoons of ginger
- 1 lettuce (washed)
- 2 tbsp rice wine
- 2 tablespoons of oil

* 1 teaspoon miso paste
* 1 teaspoon honey
* 1 teaspoon of water

* 2 avocados (peeled, pitted and cut)
* Pinch of salt

Preparation:

1. Make the dressing with a food processor by mixing together the carrots, ginger, rice wine, oil, miso paste, honey and water.

2. Divide the salad between four plates. Place the avocado and cucumber on top.

3. Sprinkle a little salt over each salad and distribute the dressing evenly.

Soy coated shishito peppers

Preparation time: 20 minutes, servings: 4

Nutritional information: calories: 267 kcal, carbohydrates: 29 g, fat: 12.2 g, protein: 5.5 g

Ingredients:

* 225 g shishito peppers
* 1 tbsp oi l
* 2 teaspoons of salt

* 1 tbsp lemon juice
* 1 tsp Shichimi Togarashi (7 spice powder)

For the sauce
* 2 tbsp soy sauce
* 1 teaspoon honey
* 1 teaspoon lemon juice

* 1 teaspoon of finely chopped ginger
* 1 teaspoon finely chopped green onion

Preparation:

1. Mix all the ingredients for the sauce in a small bowl.

2. Heat the oil in a pan.

3. When the pan is hot, add the peppers and reduce the heat.

4. Fry the peppers for 5 minutes, then add the sauce. Turn them over regularly and cook for another 5-12 minutes.

5. Take the finished peppers out of the pan and sprinkle salt, lemon juice and Shichimi Togarashi over them.

Avocado salad

Preparation time: 5 minutes, servings: 4

Nutritional information: calories: 1262 kcal, carbohydrates: 15 g, fat: 119 g, protein: 16.6 g

Ingredients:

* 1 tbsp oil
* 1 teaspoon sesame oil

* 2 tbsp rice wine
* 2 tbsp mirin

- 1 teaspoon chopped ginger
- 1 teaspoon of suga r
- 250-500 g lettuce leaves (washed

- 2 avocados (peeled, pitted and cut)
- 2 tbsp toasted sesame seeds

Preparation:

1. For the dressing, mix the oil, sesame oil, rice wine, mirin, ginger and sugar in a small bowl.
2. Mix the lettuce leaves with the dressing in a large bowl and divide it between four plates.
3. Divide the avocado on the plates and sprinkle with salt and sesame seeds.

Spicy Bean Sprouts Salad

Preparation time: 10 minutes, servings: 4

Nutritional information: calories: 343 kcal, carbohydrates: 13 g, fat: 22 g, protein: 14.3 g

Ingredients:

- 250 g of bean sprouts
- 1 tbsp sesame oil
- 1 tbsp oil
- 2 teaspoons of soy sauce
- 1 tsp Shichimi Togarashi (7 spice powder)

- Pinch of salt
- 45 g spring onions (finely chopped)
- 2 tbsp toasted sesame seeds
- 1.4 liters of water

Preparation:

1. Heat the water in a large saucepan.
2. Cook the bean sprouts in it for 1-2 minutes. Drain the bean sprouts and pour cold water over them.
3. Mix the sesame oil, soy sauce, shichimi togarashi and salt in a bowl.
4. Add the bean sprouts and mix everything well.
5. Divide the salad between four plates and sprinkle with spring onions and sesame seeds.

Pickled cucumbers

Preparation time: 5 minutes + 4 hours, servings: 6

Nutritional information: calories: 174 kcal, carbohydrates: 19 g, fat: 7 g, protein: 8 g

Ingredients:

- 2 cucumbers (thinly sliced)
- 1 tbsp salt

- 1 teaspoon toasted sesame seeds
- Kombu (approx. 5 cm, washed)

Preparation:

1. Mix the cucumbers with the salt in a bowl. Add the sesame seeds and mix well.
2. Arrange the cucumbers in the bowl so that the slices lie flat in the bowl. Place kombu on top and place a plate over it. Weigh down the plate and put the bowl in the refrigerator for 4 hours.
3. Remove the kombu before serving.

Gomare (spinach)

Preparation time: 10 minutes, servings: 4

Nutritional information: calories: 439 kcal, carbohydrates: 31 g, fat: 23.5 g, protein: 19.2 g

Ingredients:
- 450 g of fresh spinach
- 1 teaspoon toasted sesame seeds
- 1 teaspoon of sugar
- 2 teaspoons of soy sauce

Preparation:
1. Heat a saucepan of water and bring it to a boil.
2. Prepare an ice bath for the spinach.
3. Heat a pan and add the sesame seeds. Wait about 1 minute. Put the sesame seeds in a mortar and grind them.
4. Mix the sesame seeds, sugar and soy sauce in a small bowl.
5. When the water boils, add the spinach for 30-45 seconds. Take it out of the water with a slotted spoon and place it in the ice bath. Drain well and squeeze out.
6. Mix the spinach with the sauce.

Fried eggplant, mushrooms and peppers with miso

Preparation time: 15 minutes, servings: 4

Nutritional information: calories: 383.2 kcal, carbohydrates: 28.2 g, fat: 23 g, protein: 16 g

Ingredients:
- 2 tbsp white miso paste
- 2 tbsp mirin
- 2 tbsp soy sauce
- 1 tbsp oil
- 1 tbsp sesame oil
- 2 eggplants (finely chopped)
- 2 trumpet mushrooms (finely chopped)
- 1 red pepper (pitted and cut)

Preparation:
1. Mix the mirin, miso paste, and soy sauce in a small bowl.

2. In a large pan, heat the oil. When it's hot, add the sesame oil, mushrooms, eggplant, and peppers. Fry everything for about 5 minutes, stirring well.

3. Add the sauce, mix everything well and wait another 2 minutes.

Crispy squid

Preparation time: 15 minutes, servings: 4

Nutritional information: calories: 1603 kcal, carbohydrates: 161 g, fat: 58.4 g, protein: 103 g

Ingredients:

- Oil for deep-frying
- 150 g of flour
- 50 g potato flour
- 1 egg
- 100 ml of ice water
- 450 g of squid rings & tentacles
- 1 tsp Shichimi Togarashi (7 spice powder)
- salt

Preparation:

1. Heat the oil in a large saucepan. The oil should cover at least 4 cm.
2. Mix the flour and potato flour in a bowl.
3. In another bowl, mix the ice water and egg. Add the egg mixture to the flour and knead everything well.
4. Test whether the oil is hot by adding a drop of batter. If it sizzles right away, the oil is hot enough.
5. Turn the squid in the batter and then fry it until it is brown and crispy for about 45 seconds.
6. Place the squid on paper towels and sprinkle with shichimi togarashi.

Roasted eggplant, asparagus and peppers

Preparation time: 15 minutes, servings: 4

Nutritional information: calories: 364 kcal, carbohydrates: 36.2 g, fat: 13.7 g, protein: 22.5 g

Ingredients:

- 2 tbsp white miso paste
- 2 tbsp mirin
- 2 tbsp soy sauce
- 1 tbsp oil
- 1 tbsp sesame oil
- 2 eggplants (finely chopped)
- 400 g green asparagus (roughly cut)
- 1 red pepper (pitted and cut)

Preparation:

1. Mix the mirin, miso paste, and soy sauce in a small bowl.

2. In a large pan, heat the oil. When it's hot, add the sesame oil, asparagus, eggplant, and peppers. Fry everything for about 5 minutes, stirring well.

3. Add the sauce, mix everything well and wait another 2 minutes.

Tamagoyaki (Japanese omelette)

Preparation time: 10 minutes, servings: 4

Nutritional information **:** calories: 300.8 kcal, carbohydrates: 10.3 g, fat: 20.5 g, protein: 18.2 g

Ingredients:

- 3 eggs
- 1 spring onion (sliced)
- 1 teaspoon soy sauce
- 1 teaspoon of sugar
- Pinch of salt
- 1 teaspoon coconut oil

Preparation:

1. Whisk the eggs with the spring onions, soy sauce, sugar, and salt

2. Heat a pan over medium heat and add the coconut oil.

3. When the pan is called, add about a quarter of the egg mixture to the pan so that the bottom of the pan is thinly covered.

4. Use chopsticks to roll up the hardened egg. Put about a quarter of the egg mixture back into the pan. Lift the omelette to distribute the egg mixture underneath.

5. Repeat rolling and adding egg mixture until used.

6. Remove the omelette roll from the pan, let it cool before serving, and cut it into pieces.

Menma (spiced bamboo shoots)

Preparation time: 30 minutes, servings: 12

Nutritional information **:** calories: 237.3 kcal, carbohydrates: 16.2 g, fat: 10.6 g, protein: 13.4 g

Ingredients:

- 455 g fresh bamboo shoot s
- 1 tbsp sesame oil
- 475 ml of water
- 3 teaspoons of dashi granules
- 1 tbsp soy sauce
- 1 tbsp sake
- 2 teaspoons of sugar
- 1 teaspoon salt

Preparation:

1. Cut the bamboo shoots in half, then into thin slices.

2. Put the sesame oil, water, dashi granules, soy sauce, sake, sugar and salt in a large pan and heat on medium heat. Then add the bamboo shoots

3. Let everything cook with the lid open for about 20 minutes until the bamboo shoots have absorbed most of the liquid.

Poached eggs

Preparation time: 10 minutes, servings: number of eggs

Nutritional information: calories: 83.8 kcal, carbohydrates: 0.6 g, fat: 6.5 g, protein: 5.7 g

Ingredients:

• eggs
• Some white wine or lemon juice

Preparation:

1. Fill a medium saucepan with water so that it covers about 3.5 cm. Bring it to a boil and add wine or lemon juice. This helps the eggs clot faster but be careful: Too much and the eggs taste sour. When the water is boiling, reduce the heat so it simmer.
2.   Beat an egg into a small mold or cup. Quickly and carefully add them to the boiling water. Boil the egg for about 3.5 minutes.
3. Remove the egg with a slotted spoon and dry it with a paper towel.

Chashu (boiled pork)

Preparation time: 4 ½ hours, servings: 4 - 6

Nutritional information **:** calories: 4315.5 kcal, carbohydrates: 559 g, fat: 119 g, protein: 251 g

Ingredients:

• 900 g pork shoulder (or other part with fat, cut into approx. 10-13 cm pieces and rolled into a roll fixed with threads)
• 2.8 liters of water
• 946 ml soy sauce
• 500 g of sugar
• 175 ml Mirin (sweet rice wine)
• 1 spring onion (sliced)
• 1 tbsp ginger (grated)

Preparation:

1. Add the rolled pork shoulder, water, soy sauce, sugar, mirin, spring onion, and ginger to a large saucepan and bring to a boil. Then reduce the heat and let it simmer for about 4 hours. Skim off the foam.
2. Take the meat out of the liquid. Check whether it is done by sticking a wooden stick into the meat. If nothing sticks, it's done.
3. Let the meat soak in a little roasting liquid in the refrigerator overnight.
4. Do not throw away the liquid! You can z. Use for example for marinated half eggs (recipe on page 25) or Menma (see page 52).
5. Before using the meat for the ramen soup, sear it on all sides in a pan for about 1-2 minutes. This will make the meat nice and crispy. Cut it into pieces about 6 mm in size.

Toasted nori (seaweed)

Preparation time: 2 minutes, servings: 2 rectangles each

Nutritional information: calories: 10 kcal, carbohydrates: 4 g, fat: 0 g, protein: 3 g

Ingredients:

- Japanese nori sheets
- sesame oil
- sea salt

Preparation:

1. Rub both sides of the nori sheet with sesame oil.
2. Toast the nori sheets over a small flame (e.g. a gas stove) until they are crispy.
3. Sprinkle salt over each nori sheet and place 4 to 5 on top of each other.
4. With a sharp knife, cut the pile into quarters.

Beni Shoga (pickled ginger)

Preparation time: 2 weeks, servings: 30

Nutritional information **:** calories: 570.8 kcal, carbohydrates: 124 g, fat: 5.1 g, protein: 6 g

Ingredients:

- 170 g of fresh ginger
- 235 g umeboshi (pickled Japanese plums)
- 2 tablespoons of sal t
- 4 tablespoons of sugar
- 4 tbsp Mirin (sweet rice wine)
- 1 teaspoon yellow mustard seeds

Preparation:

1. Peel the ginger and cut it into pieces about 6 mm in size.
2. Put the umeboshi, salt, sugar, mirin and mustard seeds in a small mason jar. Screw it on and shake it vigorously.
3. Add the ginger and put in the refrigerator for 2 weeks.
4. Take the ginger out of the jar and cut it into very small strips.

Ajitsuke Tamago (marinated eggs)

Preparation time: 1 ½ hours + 2 days, servings: 6

Nutritional information **:** calories: 1952 kcal, carbohydrates: 263.5 g, fat: 130 g, protein: 42.6 g

Ingredients:

- 235 ml soy sauce
- 200 g of sugar
- 1 ½ TE ginger (grated)
- 1 TE garlic (chopped)
- 120 ml Mirin (sweet rice wine)
- 6 eggs

- ½ cup bonito flakes

Preparation:

1. Heat a large saucepan and add the soy sauce, sugar, ginger, and garlic. When the mixture starts bubbling, remove it from the stove and add mirin. Let the whole thing cool down.
2. Bring water to a boil in a saucepan. Put the eggs in and let them cook for about 6 ½ minutes. After that, scare them off and let them cool down.
3. Take a well-sealable box, put the eggs in it, 700 ml of water and 235 ml of the prepared sauce. The eggs should be completely covered. Place a paper towel over it and place the bonito flakes on top. Put the box in the refrigerator for 2 days.
4. Remove the eggs from the sauce and cut them in half.

Kakuni (braised pork belly)

Preparation time: 4 hours, servings: 6

Nutritional information **:** calories: 3865.6 kcal, carbohydrates: 636 g, fat: 113 g, protein: 98.2 g

Ingredients:

- 455 g pork belly (boneless, cut into large pieces)
- 2.8 liters of water
- 946 ml soy sauce
- 500 g of sugar
- 175 Mirin (sweet rice wine)
- 1 clove of garlic (peeled)
- 1 spring onion (roughly chopped)
- 1 tbsp ginger (chopped)

Preparation:

1. Bring the water to a boil and add the meat, soy sauce, sugar, mirin, garlic, spring onion and ginger. Reduce the heat and simmer for 4 hours.
2. Take the meat out of the liquid. Check whether it is done by sticking a wooden stick into the meat. If nothing sticks, it's done.
3. Let the meat soak in a little liquid overnight. You can use the remaining liquid for. Use it e.g. for Ajitsuke Tamago (marinated eggs) on page 25 or for the classic Shoyu broth.
4. Before using the meat for the ramen soup, sear it on all sides in a pan for about 1-2 minutes. This will make the meat nice and crispy. Cut it into small pieces.

Mayu (black garlic oil)

Preparation time: 10 minutes, servings: 12 (120 ml)

Nutritional information: calories: 541.7 kcal, carbohydrates: 0.3 g, fat: 61 g, protein: 0.1 g

Ingredients:

- 60 ml of avocado oil
- 8 cloves of garlic (chopped)

• 60 ml sesame oil

Preparation:

1. Heat the avocado oil in a small saucepan. Add the garlic and cook until it turns dark brown. Reduce the heat and wait for the garlic to turn black.

2. Put the mixture in a blender along with the sesame oil. Mix everything well.

Aji-Moyashi (marinated bean sprouts)

Preparation time: 6 minutes, servings: 5

Nutritional information: calories: 406 kcal, carbohydrates: 21.3 g, fat: 23.8 g, protein: 21.6 g

Ingredients:

- 340 g bean sprouts
- 1 tbsp sesame (toasted)
- 2 tbsp sesame oil
- 1 ½ tsp soy sauc e
- 1 ½ tsp Shichimi Togarashi (7 spice powder)
- Pinch of salt
- Pinch of pepper

Preparation:

1. Bring a large saucepan of water to a boil and cook the bean sprouts for 1-2 minutes. Then pour them off.

2. Put all the other ingredients in a large enough bowl and stir. Add the cooked bean sprouts.

Toasted garlic butter

Preparation time: 1 ¼ hours, servings: 12 (120 ml)

Nutritional information: calories: 679.3 kcal, carbohydrates: 29.3 g, fat: 59 g, protein: 6.5 g

Ingredients:

- 1 bulb of garlic
- salt and pepper (as required)
- olive oil
- 55 g unsalted butter

Preparation:

1. Preheat the oven to 200 ° C.

2. Cut off the top piece (approx. 6 mm) of the garlic bulb and place it on aluminum foil. Cover the tuber with olive oil, salt and pepper and wrap it completely in the aluminum foil.

3. Bake the tuber in the oven for an hour, until the toes protrude and the skin turns a light brown. Take out the tuber and let it cool.

4. Peel the tuber then mash the toes into a paste.
5. Put the garlic paste in a bowl and add the butter. Mix everything well.

Garlic chips

Preparation time: 8 minutes, servings: 10

Nutritional information: calories: 181.2 kcal, carbohydrates: 11.4 g, fat: 13.8 g, protein: 2.4 g

Ingredients:

• olive oil (for frying)
• 5 cloves of garlic (peeled, thinly sliced)

Preparation:

1. Pour as much olive oil into a small saucepan that covers about 1/2 inch of the saucepan and heat it over medium heat. Prepare a plate covered with a paper towel.
2. Put a slice of garlic in the hot oil. If it sizzles right away, the oil is hot enough. Add the garlic slices in two passes for 5-8 seconds each. Be careful, the garlic will burn quickly & then turn bitter.
3. Remove the garlic with a slotted spoon and let it drain on the paper towel and cool.

Spicy pork

Preparation time: 15 minutes, servings: 4

Nutritional information **:** calories: 627.2 kcal, carbohydrates: 8.3g, fat: 14g, protein: 113.5g

Ingredients:

• 500 g minced pork
• ½ teaspoon salt
• 2 tbsp chili flakes

• 1 clove of garlic (peeled and grated)
• 1 teaspoon soy sauce

Preparation:

1. Heat one pan and fry the minced meat and salt vigorously in it for about 5 minutes.
2. Mix in the garlic and chili flakes and wait another minute. Finally add the soy sauce.

Roasted onions

Preparation time: 10 minutes, servings: 8

Nutritional information: calories: 258 kcal, carbohydrates: 11.3 g, fat: 21.4 g, protein: 3 g

Ingredients:

• 475 ml olive oil (for frying)

• 1 red onion (peeled, halved, sliced)

• salt (as required)

Preparation:

1. Put the olive oil in a medium saucepan. At least about 1.25 cm of the pot should be covered. Heat the saucepan over medium heat. Prepare a plate covered with a paper towel.
2. Put a slice of onion in the hot oil. If it sizzles right away, the oil is hot enough. Add the onion slices in several passes for about 15 seconds each. Be careful, the onions can burn quickly.
3. Remove the onions with a slotted spoon and let them drain on the paper towel and cool.
4. Lightly season the onions with salt.

Fried potatoes

Preparation time: 10 minutes, servings: 8

Nutritional information: calories: 437.7 kcal, carbohydrates: 13.6 g, fat: 41.5 g, protein: 1.6 g

Ingredients:

• 475 ml olive oil (for frying)
• 1 potato (floury, skin-on, thinly sliced)
• salt (as required)

Preparation:

1. Put the olive oil in a medium saucepan. At least about 1.25 cm of the pot should be covered. Heat the saucepan over medium heat. Prepare a plate covered with a paper towel.
2. Put a potato slice in the hot oil. If it sizzles right away, the oil is hot enough. Give the potato slices in several passes for about 15 seconds each. Be careful, the potatoes can burn quickly.
3. Remove the potato slices with a slotted spoon and let them drain on the paper towel and cool.
4. Lightly season the potatoes with salt.

Menma (marinated bamboo shoots)

Preparation time: 70 minutes, servings: 4

Nutritional information: calories: 1095 kcal, carbohydrates: 24 g, fat: 103 g, protein: 9 g

Ingredients:

• 300 g bamboo sprouts
• 500 ml chashu broth
• 500 ml of water
• 7 tbsp chili oil

Preparation:

1. **Pickled whole bamboo shoots** : Wash the shoots thoroughly under running water. Use a sharp kitchen knife to remove the end piece and tip. Then halve the sprouts lengthways. Now lay the halves on the cut sides and cut them horizontally into long strips.

   Dried bamboo shoots : Soak the bamboo strips in plenty of cold water for six hours. Replace the water at least three times during the soaking time.

   Fresh bamboo shoots : First, carry out the same work steps as for the pickled bamboo shoots. Then cook the bamboo strips in salted water for ten minutes. Then wash the bamboo shoots thoroughly in a kitchen strainer under cold running water.

2. In a medium saucepan, bring all ingredients to a boil over medium heat.

3. Let it simmer for about an hour, uncovered, until most of the stock has boiled down.

Tomorokoshi (marinated corn)

Preparation time: 10 minutes, servings: 3

Nutritional information **:** calories: 1623.4 kcal, carbohydrates: 275.8 g, fat: 16 g, protein: 34 g

Ingredients:

- 3 ears of corn
- 1 teaspoon rapeseed oil
- 3 tsp soy sauce
- 1 teaspoon of sugar

Preparation:

1. Blanch the corn on the cob for about 3 minutes in a large saucepan of boiling water.

2. Put the rapeseed oil in a pan over medium heat. Fry the corn on the cob until nicely browned on all sides.

3. Mix the soy sauce and sugar in a small bowl and pour it over the corn on the cob in the pan.

Horenso Gomare (Japanese sesame leaf spinach)

Preparation time: 40 minutes + 2 hours, servings: 4

Nutritional information **:** calories: 889.6 kcal, carbohydrates: 53.7 g, fat: 52.8 g, protein: 36.1 g

Ingredients:

- 1 kg of spinach
- 8 tbsp soy sauce
- 1 teaspoon sesame seeds
- 1 teaspoon sesame oil
- 1 teaspoon rapeseed oil

Preparation:

1. Clean the spinach and remove the stalks.
2. Heat the two oils in a pan. Steam the spinach in it for about 10 minutes and add the soy sauce.
3. Put everything in a sealable box, sprinkle the sesame seeds over it and let it marinate in the fridge for two hours.

Narutomaki (fish cake)

Preparation time: 2 hours, servings: 4

Nutritional information: calories: 172 kcal, carbohydrates: 31.8 g, fat: 0.3 g, protein: 2.2 g

Ingredients:
- 450 g fish fillets (waxy, e.g. pangasius)
- 100 ml water (cold)
- 10 g rice flour
- 10 g cornstarch
- 12 grams of salt
- 4 tbsp sake (rice wine)
- 1 tbsp Mirin (sweet rice wine)

For coloring:
- 80 g beetroot (cooked)
- 100 ml of water
- 1 dash of rice vinegar
- 5 g rice flour
- 1 tbsp soy sauce

Preparation:
1. The fish fillet should be ice cold when processed.
2. Put the fish together with the rice wine, soy sauce and the cold water in the food processor in portions until everything has been processed into a smooth mass. Mix in the cornstarch, rice flour and salt. Let the dough rest for half an hour
3. For the typical color swirl, spread two thirds of the mass with a wide, cold knife on a piece of greased aluminum foil.
4. Puree the cooked beetroot, rice flour, and soy sauce in the food processor and mix everything with the rest of the mixture. Spread this on the white fish mass. Leave something free at the front and back.
5. Now roll up the layers of dough (similar to rolling sushi).
6. Steam the roll for about 1 hour at 100 ° C in the oven.

Crispy hot pork

Preparation time: 15 minutes, servings: 4

Nutritional information: calories: 1098 kcal, carbohydrates: 16.2 g, fat: 75 g, protein: 88.3 g

Ingredients:
- 500 g minced pork
- 2 tbsp butter

- 2 spring onions (finely chopped)
- 2 tbsp ginger (grated)
- 1 clove of garlic (peeled and grated)

- 2 tbsp doubanjiang (fermented chili bean paste)
- 1 tbsp sesame oil
- 2 tbsp soy sauce

Preparation:

1. Heat the butter in the pan and fry the minced meat, spring onions, ginger and garlic vigorously.

2. Mix in the chili bean paste, sesame oil and soy sauce.

Ginger pork

Preparation time: 15 minutes, servings: 4

Nutritional information **:** calories: 550.6 kcal, carbohydrates: 2.9g, fat: 10.3g, protein: 110g

Ingredients:

- 500 g minced pork
- ½ teaspoon salt
- 2 tbsp ginger (grated)

- 1 clove of garlic (peeled and grated)
- 1 teaspoon soy sauce

Preparation:

1. Heat one pan and fry the minced meat and salt vigorously in it for about 5 minutes.

2. Mix in the garlic and ginger and wait another minute. Finally add the soy sauce.

Kohakutou (edible jewels)

Preparation time: 20 minutes + 4 hours

Nutritional information: calories: 2935 kcal, carbohydrates: 727 g, fat: 0.4 g, protein: 4.8 g

Ingredients:

- 400 ml of water
- 13 g agar-agar
- 650 g of sugar

- 10 tbsp fruit syrup
- 10 drops of vanilla extract
- food coloring

Preparation:

1. Boil the water together with the agar-agar powder. Add the vanilla extract and stir in the sugar. Cook the whole thing for 3 minutes.

2. Fill several small vessels with some fruit syrup and a few drops of food coloring. Pour in the hot agar-agar mixture and stir well. Let it cool and solidify in the refrigerator.

3. Loosen the mass from the molds and cut into pieces of any size.

Match ice cream (green tea ice cream)

Preparation time: 10 minutes + 1 hour, servings: 8

Nutritional information: calories: 1688 kcal, carbohydrates: 219.8 g, fat: 75 g, protein: 33.4 g

Ingredients:

- 500 ml of cream
- 500 ml Milh
- 175 g of sugar
- 1 pinch of salt
- 17 g green powder tea (matcha)

Preparation:

1. Mix all the ingredients together until the sugar has dissolved.
2. Let it freeze in the ice cream maker (about 30-40 minutes).
3. Place in the freezer for about 1 hour.

Japanese coconut jelly

Preparation time: 5 minutes + 1 day

Nutritional information: calories: 1670 kcal, carbohydrates: 155 g, fat: 108g, protein: 10.7 g

Ingredients:

- 1 can of coconut milk
- 500 ml of water
- 250 ml of oat milk
- 70 g coconut flakes
- 120 g of sugar
- 12 g agar agar

Preparation:

1. Pour coconut milk, oat milk and water together in a saucepan.
2. Stir in the sugar and agar agar. Let it boil and simmer for 3 minutes. Add the coconut flakes.
3. Pour it into a mold and leave it in the refrigerator overnight.
4. Now the jelly can be cut into cubes.

Shiratama-Dango (sticky rice balls with sesame sauce)

Preparation time: 25 minutes + 1 hour, servings: 4

Nutritional information: calories: 1059 kcal, carbohydrates: 61.1 g, fat: 0.3 g, protein: 0.7 g

Ingredients:

- 100 g glutinous rice flour
- 50 ml of water
- 3 tablespoons of sesame seeds
- 3 tablespoons of brown sugar
- 2 tbsp honey
- 1 teaspoon soy sauce
- Grated zest of one lemon

Preparation:

1. Mix together sticky rice flour and water and knead it well. The dough shouldn't get too soft.

2. Shape the dough into walnut-sized balls and flatten a little. Cook the balls in boiling water until they rise to the top. Then drain and let cool. Warning: balls are very sticky!

3. Mortar the sesame seeds. Mix sugar, honey and soy sauce with 3 tablespoons of water and briefly boil it all. Warning: burns quickly!

4. Stir the sauce well and let it cool down.

5. Optionally, you can put the balls on a skewer. Serve the sticky rice balls garnished with sauce, sesame seeds and lemon zest.

Japanese soufflé cheesecake

Preparation time: 3 hours + 4 hours, servings: 1 cake

Nutritional information : calories: 2938 kcal, carbohydrates: 301.3 g, fat: 154 g, protein: 83 g

Ingredients:

- 300 g of cream cheese
- 100 ml of milk
- 50 g butter
- 6 eggs
- 2 tablespoons of lemon juice
- 160 g of sugar
- 1 packet of vanilla sugar
- 60 g of flour
- 20 g cornstarch
- 1 pinch of salt
- 3 tbsp apricot jam

Preparation:

1. Preheat the oven (top and bottom heat) to 160 °. Pour approx. 2 cm of water into a slightly deeper baking sheet.

2. Butter a 26 mm springform pan, line it with baking paper and butter it. The baking paper must protrude approx. 5 cm over the edge. Wrap the lower outer part of the pan with aluminum foil to ensure that no water gets on the cake.

3. Warm the milk and butter and let the cream cheese melt in it over low heat. Stir everything well. Separate the eggs and add the yolks along with the flour and starch to the mixture.

4. Briefly whip the egg whites with the salt. Add sugar, vanilla sugar and lemon juice and keep beating until the sugar has dissolved and the mixture is very stiff. Beat the ice snow for another minute on a low setting to get a particularly fine-pored ice snow.

5. Carefully lift the ice snow under the mass. Put the dough in the tin, cover the tin with aluminum foil and place it in the tray filled with water.

6. Bake the cake for 70 minutes. Then remove the aluminum foil and bake it for another 5 - 10 minutes until it gets some color.

7. Turn off the oven but keep the ventilation running. After 10 minutes, open the oven door a crack and let it stand in the oven for 30 to 60 minutes. This is very important so that the cake does not collapse.

8. Turn the cake out of the pan and let it cool down.

Japanese Christmas cake

Preparation time: 1 hour, servings: 1 cake

Nutritional information: calories: 2130 kcal, carbohydrates: 234 g, fat: 118.5 g, protein: 28 g

Ingredients:

- 70 g rice flour
- 4 eggs
- 120 g of sugar
- 3 tablespoons of water
- 2 tablespoons of oil

- 1 tsp baking powder
- 300 m of cream
- strawberries
- bananas

Upon need:
- food coloring
- fruit

- Decor

Preparation:

1. Separate the ones. Mix the egg yolks with 35 g sugar and beat them until frothy. Add water and oil.

2. Mix together rice flour and baking powder. Sift the flour into the egg yolk mixture and mix everything into a dough.

3. Beat the egg whites with 35 g sugar until stiff and fold the egg whites into the batter.

4. Put the dough in a size 16 springform pan and bake everything at 180 ° C for 30 - 40 minutes. If necessary, place a sheet of baking paper over the pan if the cake turns too brown.

5. Mix the cream and sugar and beat it until stiff (if necessary color with food coloring).

6. Halve the cooled cake base lengthways and brush it with the cream.

7. Chop strawberries and bananas and spread them on the cake base. Put the other half on it.

8. Spread the rest of the cream evenly, decorate the cake even more if necessary and put it in the refrigerator.

Gyoza with fruit filling

Preparation time: 1 ¼ hours, servings: 5

Nutritional information: calories: 2003 kcal, carbohydrates: 164.3 g, fat: 122g, protein: 7.7 g

Ingredients:

- 20 sheets of pastry (gyoza sheets)
- 2 plum s
- 80 ml of Armagnac
- 1 peach
- 80 g of sugar
- 30 g butter
- 1 tbsp cornstarch
- 80 g clarified butter

Preparation:

1. Let the plums for the filling simmer in a small saucepan with the Armagnac for a few minutes so that the alcohol can soak into the fruit.
2. Let everything cool, remove the pips from the plums and cut the pulp into small cubes.
3. Cut the peach crosswise and briefly put it in boiling water. The skin can now be peeled off very easily. Core the peach and cut it into thin slices.
4. Melt the butter in a large pan and fry the peach with the sugar in it until the slices are coated with dark caramel. Then dice the peach and add it to the plum.
5. Mix the starch with some water. Lay out the gyoza leaves and place a teaspoon of the fruit mixture in the center of each. Coat half of the edge of the dough with the starch mixture, fold it up and press the edge tightly.
6. Heat the clarified butter in a pan. Put in the gyoza bags in portions and only let them brown lightly on one side. Add two spoons of water and immediately put the lid on the pan. Let it steam for 3 - 4 minutes. When the top has become translucent, fry it again for a minute without the lid.

Japanese sesame chocolate cake

Preparation time: 5 minutes + 1 day

Nutritional information: calories: 5582 kcal, carbohydrates: 585 g, fat: 320 g, protein: 91.2 g

Ingredients:

For the ground:
- 50 g butter
- 50 g of white chocolate
- 100 g flour
- 2 egg yolks
- 100 g of sugar
- 1 pinch of salt
- 1 tbsp ground almonds

For the sesame mixture:

- 150 g black sesame seeds
- 100 g butter
- 250 grams of sugar

For the glaze:
- 150 g dark chocolate (70% cocoa)
- 25 g butter

- 50 g flour
- 2 eggs (whisked)
- 1 pinch of baking powder

- 50 ml of cream

Preparation:

1. For the bottom, melt the white chocolate and butter. Mix in the almonds and flour. Beat the egg yolks with the sugar and add a pinch of salt.

2. Line a loaf pan (max. 20 cm long and 10 cm wide) with baking paper. Put the liquid dough in and bake it at 160 ° C for 12-15 minutes.

3. Meanwhile, for the sesame mixture, melt the butter together with the sesame seeds in a saucepan. Stir in the sugar and egg and work in the flour and baking powder.

4. Carefully lift the bottom out of the mold and fill the mold again with the sesame mixture. Bake them at 180 ° C for about 35 minutes. Take the mold out of the oven and let everything cool down.

5. Take the sesame mixture out of the mold, put the first base back into the mold and the sesame base over it. Lightly press the bottoms.

6. Melt the dark chocolate in the cream and mix in the butter. Let the mass cool down so that it is nice and viscous and pour the mass over the top of the cake. Coat it evenly and thickly.

7. Put the cake in the cold for at least 2 hours. Remove from the mold to serve.

Sesame pudding with fruits

Preparation time: 1 ¼ hours, servings: 8

Nutritional information: calories: 1700 kcal, carbohydrates: 146.2 g, fat: 96g, protein:

51 g

Ingredients:

- 1 glass of sesame paste (tahini)
- 500 ml of milk
- 4 tablespoons of sugar

- ½ tsp agar agar
- 500 g fruits (e.g. berries, pineapples, grapes, apples ...)

Preparation:

1. Heat 400ml of the milk and set 100ml aside. Add the tahini and sugar to the hot milk, wait until everything has dissolved.

2. Mix the agar-agar into the milk you have set aside and stir it into the sesame milk. Rinse a sufficiently large bowl with hot water and add the mixture.

3. Use two tablespoons to cut small portions out of the mass and serve garnished with fruit.

Matcha tiramisu

Preparation time: 30 minutes + 5 hours, servings: 8

Nutritional information: calories: 2676 kcal, carbohydrates: 195 g, fat: 48g, protein: 189 g

Ingredients:

For the cream:
- 3 egg yolks
- 70 g of sugar
- 2 tbsp Marsala
- 250 grams of mascarpone
- 360 ml of cream

For dusting:
- 2 tbsp matcha powder

Also:
- 2 tbsp milk
- 125 ml water (80 ° hot)
- 1 ½ tbsp match powder
- 24 ladyfingers

Preparation:

1. In a bowl, beat the egg yolks, sugar and marsala until stiff. Fold in the mascarpone. In a separate bowl, whip the cream until stiff.
2. Stir the 1 ½ tablespoons matcha powder into the hot water until there are no lumps left. Stir in the milk. Dip the sponge fingers in the milk tea and lay out a mold (approx. 20 x 20 cm) with it.
3. Spread half of the cream on top. Put another layer of ladyfingers and spread the rest of the cream on top.
4. Put the tiramisu in the refrigerator for at least 5 hours. Before serving, sprinkle the 2 tablespoons of match powder on top.

Ginger jelly with passion fruit sauce

Preparation time: 35 minutes + 6 hours, servings: 4

Nutritional information: calories: 430 kcal, carbohydrates: 88.5 g, fat: 3g, protein: 10.7 g

Ingredients:

- 25 g ginger (finely chopped)
- 1 stick of lemongrass (roughly cut)
- 2 sheets of white gelatin
- 2 sheets of red gelatin
- 250 ml of water
- 30 grams of sugar
- 1 bag of tea
- 4 tbsp grenadine
- 2 tablespoons of lime juice

For the sauce:
- 6 passion fruits
- 100 ml orange juice (freshly squeezed)
- 30 grams of sugar

Preparation:

1. Soak the gelatin in water.
2. Boil the water together with ginger, sugar and lemongrass and let it steep for 30 minutes. Pour the liquid through a sieve and heat it again.
3. Add the tea bag and let it steep for another 4 minutes.
4. Dissolve the gelatin in the liquid and add the grenadine and lime juice.
5. Pour the liquid into a baking dish (approx. 3 cm high, 400 ml capacity) lined with cling film. Put the mold in the refrigerator and let it set.
6. Cut the passion fruits in half and scrape them off. Add the orange juice and puree everything. Pour the sauce through a sieve, add the sugar and bring to a simmer in a saucepan until the sugar has dissolved. Let the sauce cool down.
7. Take the mold out of the refrigerator and cut everything into large cubes. Serve with sauce.

Sesame cream with sugar syrup

Preparation time: 25 minutes + 3 hours, servings: 6

Nutritional information: calories: 1382 kcal, carbohydrates: 168 g, fat: 60g, protein: 38.6 g

Ingredients:
- 500 ml of milk
- 3 tablespoons of sugar
- 80 g sesame seeds
- 3 ½ sheets of gelatin

For the syrup:
- 2 tablespoons of brown sugar
- 4 tbsp white sugar
- 100 ml of water

Preparation:

1. Toast the sesame seeds in a pan without oil. Using the back of a spoon, mash the sesame seeds into a paste.
2. Stir the paste into the milk, add 3 tablespoons of sugar and heat the whole thing until the sugar has dissolved.
3. Soak the gelatin in cold water, squeeze it out and add it to the sesame milk.
4. Fill the liquid into bowls and stand for min. 3 hours in the refrigerator.
5. For the syrup, heat the water and dissolve the sugar in it.
6. To serve, pour sauce over each cream and sprinkle some sesame seeds on top.

Japanese cheesecake with only 3 ingredients

Preparation time: 50 minutes + 1 hour, servings: 1 cake

Nutritional information: calories: 1762 kcal, carbohydrates: 136.7 g, fat: 119.2 g, protein: 37 g

Ingredients:

- 200 g white chocolate
- 150 g of crème fraîche
- 3 eggs

Preparation:

1. Separate the eggs and put the egg whites in the freezer.
2. Cut the chocolate into small pieces and melt them in a double boiler. Let the chocolate cool down a little.
3. Mix in the egg yolks and crème fraîche. Stir until a creamy mass has formed.
4. Take the egg white out of the freezer, beat it into the egg whites and gently fold it into the mass.
5. Put the dough in a springform pan and bake it at 180 ° C for 15 minutes. Then reduce the heat to 150 ° C and bake for another 15 minutes. Finally let it rest for 15 minutes in the switched off oven.

Japanese coffee jelly

Preparation time: 10 minutes + 6 hours, servings: 4

Nutritional information: calories: 647.3 kcal, carbohydrates: 93.3 g, fat: 25.4 g, protein: 11.3 g

Ingredients:

- 470 ml strong, hot coffee
- 1 packet of gelatin powder
- 60 g of sugar
- 100 ml of cream
- 2 tablespoons of sugar

Preparation:

1. Firstly, stir the gelatin powder in 4 teaspoons of water and let it swell for 10 minutes.
2. Add the sugar to the coffee and stir until the sugar has dissolved. Let the coffee cool down.
3. Fill the coffee into a flat dish (approx. 2 cm high) and put it in the refrigerator for 6 hours.

4. Whip the cream with 2 teaspoons of sugar.

5. Take the mold out of the refrigerator and cut everything into large cubes. Serve with cream.

Japanese style fried fruit

Preparation time: 50 minutes + 1 hour, servings: 6

Nutritional information: calories: 1458 kcal, carbohydrates: 220 g, fat: 48.7 g, protein: 26.4 g

Ingredients:

- 1 egg (including the egg white)
- 200 g of flour
- 1 pinch of salt
- 1 teaspoon of sugar
- 1 pinch of ground ginger
- 1 banana
- 1 apple
- 1 pear
- Oil for deep-frying
- powdered sugar
- 300 ml of cold water

Preparation:

1. Beat the egg whites with 300 ml of cold water until frothy.

2. Sift the flour and add salt, sugar, ginger and egg white foam. Mix everything into a runny batter and refrigerate for an hour.

3. Prepare the fruit. Halve the bananas lengthways and cut into quarters. Wash and core the pear and apple. Then cut them into slices.

4. Pour 4-5 cm high oil into a deep pan and heat it. Have paper towels ready for the finished fruit.

5. Add the fruit to the oil in portions and fry until golden brown.

6. Place them on the kitchen paper and let the fruits drain.

7. Dust the fruit with a little powdered sugar.

Melon Pan

Preparation time: 30 minutes + 1 day, servings: 5

Nutritional information: calories: 1402 kcal, carbohydrates: 221 g, fat: 41.5 g, protein: 31.7 g

Ingredients:

For the shortcrust pastry:
- 25 g butter
- 35 g of sugar
- 25 g eggs (whisked)
- 90 g of flour
- ¼ tsp baking powder

For the yeast dough:
- 140 g flour
- 25 g of sugar
- 1 teaspoon salt
- 5 ml of milk

- 3 g dry yeast
- 1 tbsp egg (quenched)
- 70 ml of warm water
- 15 g butter

Preparation:

1. First, for the shortcrust pastry, put the butter in a bowl and beat it with a whisk until frothy. Stir the sugar into the butter. Add the egg in several steps.

2. Mix the flour and baking powder in a separate bowl and stir twice before adding to the butter mixture. Knead everything well, cover the dough with cling film and put it in the refrigerator for an hour.

3. For the yeast dough, carefully mix the flour, sugar, salt, milk and dry yeast in a bowl. Add the warm water and the egg. Dust a work surface with flour and knead the sticky dough. Knead the dough until it is less sticky.

4. Press the dough flat and spread butter on it. Knead the dough for another 10 minutes.

5. Shape the dough into a ball, place it in a bowl covered with foil and let it rest for 40 minutes in a warm place.

6. After the dough has rested, divide it into 5 equal parts and knead the air out. Shape the dough into balls and let it rest for another 20 minutes.

7. Also divide the shortcrust pastry into 5 equal parts and shape it into balls. Place the balls between cling film and press them flat. The circles should have a diameter of approx. 9 cm.

8. Place the shortcrust flatbreads on a yeast dough ball and press around on the outside until everything is covered. Only the bottom of the sphere remains open. Roll each of the balls in sugar and cut the shortcrust pastry into a diamond shape.

9. Let the balls rest for another 40 minutes and then bake them for 10-12 minutes at 170 ° C until they are lightly browned.

Red bean paste

Preparation time: 30 minutes + 1 day, servings: 1

Nutritional information: calories: 1095 kcal, carbohydrates: 262 g, fat: 0.6 g, protein: 6 g

Ingredients:

- 250 g azuki beans
- 250 grams of sugar

- 1 pinch of salt

Preparation:

1. Soak the beans overnight.
2. Boil the beans in a saucepan with plenty of water for about 1 ½ hours.

3. Drain the beans and press the finished beans through a sieve.
4. Put the beans in a saucepan, cover with water and add salt and sugar. Boil the whole thing for 10 minutes over low heat, stirring well.

Ichigo Daifuku (sweet sticky rice balls)

Preparation time: 4 minutes + 1 hour, servings: 10

Nutritional information: calories: 1095 kcal, carbohydrates: 262 g, fat: 0.6 g, protein: 6 g

Ingredients:

- 375 grams of flour
- 250 ml of water
- 125 g of sugar
- 1 can of Anko (sweet red bean paste)
- 10 strawberries (washed)
- starch (for powdering the hands)

Preparation:

1. In a microwave-safe container, stir together the flour, sugar and water until it is free from lumps. Put a lid on it and put it in the microwave for 4 minutes on the highest setting.
2. The dough should now be slightly transparent and have a soft consistency.
3. Flour a work surface with starch and pour the dough on it. Flatten the dough and put a strawberry in it. Cover the strawberry with batter so that it forms a closed ball.

White chocolate wasabi panna cotta

Preparation time: 15 minutes + 3 hours, servings: 8

Nutritional information: calories: 1929 kcal, carbohydrates: 93.3 g, fat: 163.2 g, protein: 21.5 g

Ingredients:

- 500 ml of cream
- 120 g white chocolate
- 2 sheets of gelatin
- 1 ½ tsp wasabi powder

Preparation:

1. Break the chocolate into pieces and melt them in the cream. Add a teaspoon of the wasabi powder and stir everything with a little water until smooth.
2. Soak the gelatin, then squeeze it out and mix it with the liquid.
3. Fill everything into small molds and put it in the refrigerator for at least 3 hours. Sprinkle with the remaining wasabi powder before serving.

Tofu cream with oranges

Preparation time: 60 minutes + 3 hours, servings: 4

Nutritional information: calories: 1058 kcal, carbohydrates: 127.7 g, fat: 45 g, protein: 27 g

Ingredients:

- 200 g of tofu
- 3 oranges
- 1 pomegranate (the seeds of it)
- 4 pickled ginger plums (diced)
- 2 rusks
- 3 cl orange liqueu r
- 2 tbsp honey
- 1 pinch of coriander
- 125 ml of cream
- 1 packet of vanilla sugar

Preparation:

1. Rub the peel of an orange and squeeze out the juice. The other oranges are peeled and one of them is diced.
2. Crumble the rusks. Put the tofu in a blender and beat it until creamy. Gradually add the orange juice, honey and liqueur. Then fold ginger plum cubes and orange cubes underneath.
3. Beat the cream together with the vanilla sugar until stiff and mix in the orange peel. Add this to the tofu cream.
4. Divide the cream on dessert bowls and serve with oranges and pomegranate seeds.

Strawberry coconut milk jelly

Preparation time: 30 minutes + 2 hours, servings: 4

Nutritional information: calories: 2960 kcal, carbohydrates: 325 g, fat: 171g, protein: 18.9 g

Ingredients:

- 400 ml coconut milk
- 30 grams of sugar
- 30 g tapioca flour

For the jelly:
- 100 g strawberries
- 300 ml coconut milk
- 30 grams of sugar
- 2 g agar aga r

For the sauce:
- 200 g strawberries
- 60 g of sugar
- 2 tablespoons of lemon juice

Preparation:

1. For the coconut butter, put the coconut milk, sugar and tapioca flour in a saucepan. Stir everything well with a whisk to avoid lumps. After the sugar has dissolved and the mixture has boiled for a moment, take the saucepan off the stove and place it in ice water.
2. Prepare the strawberry jelly by mixing the strawberries, coconut milk and sugar in a blender. Add the agar-agar and mix everything again.
3. Put the mass in a saucepan and bring to a boil. Then press the mass through a sieve into a bowl and let it cool down.
4. For the strawberry sauce, put the strawberries, sugar and lemon juice in a saucepan and let it simmer for about 10 minutes. Skim off the resulting foam with a slotted spoon. Let the sauce cool down.
5. Put everything in glasses in the following order: strawberry sauce, coconut butter, strawberry jelly. Before serving, put it in the refrigerator for at least an hour and garnish with cream and fruit.

Fried bananas with honey

Preparation time: 20 minutes, servings: 2

Nutritional information: calories: 361 kcal, carbohydrates: 41.5 g, fat: 20.3 g, protein: 2.3 g

Ingredients:

- 2 banana s
- butter
- 2 teaspoons of honey

Preparation:

1. Peel the bananas and cut them in half crosswise and then lengthways.
2. Put some butter in a pan and heat it up. Fry the banana pieces in it until they turn lightly brown. Turn the bananas over and brush them with honey.
3. Arrange on a preheated plate.

Miso caramel cream

Preparation time: 25 minutes, servings: 2

Nutritional information: calories: 2642 kcal, carbohydrates: 399 g, fat: 131.6 g, protein: 64.2 g

Ingredients:

- 360 g of sugar
- 60 ml of water
- 400 ml of cream
- 100 g of light miso paste

Preparation:

1. Dissolve the miso paste in the cream. If lumps appear, pour the cream through a sieve.

2. Heat water and sugar in a saucepan. As soon as the mixture turns golden brown, take it off the stove and carefully add the miso cream.

3. Cook everything down to the desired consistency. Make sure that the mass is thicker when it has cooled down.

Classic Tonkotsu broth

Preparation time: 4 hours, servings: 10

Nutritional information: calories: 7006 kcal, carbohydrates: 90 g, fat: 265 g, protein: 1059 g

Ingredients:

Seabura (cooked pork loin)
• 700 g saddle of pork, cut into strips
• water

Tonkotsu broth
• 225 g chicken feet (washed, skinless and toes free)
• 3.6 - 4.5 kg pork knuckle (broken, for bone marrow)

• 455 g potatoes (peeled and roughly cut)
• 4.7 liters of water

Shiodare (for the salty taste)
• 1 large rectangular piece of kombu (approx. 25 cm long, roughly cut)
• 2 small dried Shiitake mushrooms (crushed)
• 946 ml of water
• 2 teaspoons of bonito flakes

• 300 g carpet shells
• 140 g of salt

• Shoyudare (for the soy sauce flavor)
• All ingredients of Shiodare and Chashu (recipe see page 122)

Preparation:

1. Before you start, prepare chashu.

2. Start with the Seabura: put the pork loin in a saucepan and cover with water. Bring the water to a boil briefly and let it simmer for 4 hours.

3. Cooking the Tonkotsu broth: Boil the water in a separate saucepan. Blanch the chicken feet, dry them off, and place them in a pressure cooker with the pork knuckle and potatoes. Cover everything with 4.7 liters of water. Make sure the water and other ingredients don't fill more than half of your pot.

4. Heat the pot until steam escapes from the pressure valve (this can take up to 20 minutes). Wait approx. 10 minutes until the pot is filled with steam. Set the heat to the highest level and let it cook for an hour.

5. Making the Shiodare: Take a medium saucepan and bring the kombu, shiitake mushrooms and 950 ml water to a boil. Reduce the heat and were about 5 minutes.

Take out the kombu and shiitake mushrooms and transfer the liquid to a clean medium saucepan.

6.   Add the bonito flakes to the liquid, bring it to a boil. Let it simmer for 5 minutes. Squeeze the bonito flakes and remove them from the soup. Put the soup in a clean medium saucepan.

7.   Bring the soup to a boil and add the carpet clams. Let it simmer for 5 minutes. Remove the mussels with a sieve. Transfer one liter of the broth to a new saucepan and add the salt (140 g).

8.   After an hour, take the pressure cooker off the stove and release the pressure. Crush the pork bones to expose the bone marrow. Cook the whole thing on a low temperature for another hour, stirring again and again.

9.   Add one teaspoon each of chashu and shiodare to the soup bowls you plan to use with the meal.

10.   Take the saddle of pork simmering off the stove and pour off the water. Cut the meat into smaller pieces (about 5 cm). Push the whole meat piece by piece through a coarse sieve to chop it up. Seabura is ready.

11.   Strain the soup out of the pressure cooker and put it in a separate saucepan and keep it warm. Bring the soup to the boil again just before serving.

12.   Cut Chashu into 6 mm pieces and fry them in a pan until crispy.

13.   To finish your soup, add the piping hot Tonkotsu soup (235 ml) to the soup bowl. Add a teaspoon of Seabura to each serving. Add pasta and toppings as desired.

Classic Shoyu broth

Preparation time: 8-10 hours, servings: 12

Nutritional information : calories: 4919.2 kcal, carbohydrates: 84.2 g, fat: 373 g, protein: 339 g

Ingredients:

- 4 teaspoons of coconut oil
- 2 medium carrots (peeled and roughly chopped)
- ½ onion (peeled and roughly chopped)
- 3 spring onions (sliced)
- 1 apple (cored, peeled and roughly cut)
- 2 celery stalks (roughly cut)
- 5 cloves of garlic (peeled)
- 5 dried shiitake mushrooms (broken into small pieces)

- 1 whole chicken
- 4 oxtail pieces (approx. 5 cm each)
- 1 lemon (quartered)
- 2.2 liters of low-sodium chicken stoc k
- 175 ml soy sauce
- 4 tbsp dashi granules
- 2 teaspoons of salt
- ½ teaspoon white pepper
- 1 bay leaf

Preparation:

1.   Put the coconut oil, carrots, onion, apple, celery, Konoblauch and the dried Shiitake Pile in the casserole.

2. Then add the whole chicken, oxtail and lemon. Place the Dutch oven in the oven for 8-10 hours and heat it to 90 ° C. When the oxtail comes off the bone easily, it's done.

3. Use a slotted spoon to remove the coarser pieces. Strain the rest in a large saucepan. You should now have a brown, shiny, high-fat soup.

4. Bring the soup to a boil in a saucepan. Put 235 ml of the soup in each soup bowl. Add pasta and toppings as desired.

Classic Shio broth

Preparation time: 45 minutes, servings: 12

Nutritional information: calories: 515 kcal, carbohydrates: 46.5 g, fat: 29 g, protein: 10.5 g

Ingredients:

• 1 medium carrot (peeled and roughly chopped)
• ½ onion (peeled and roughly chopped)
• 3 spring onions (sliced)
• ½ apple (cored, peeled and roughly cut)
• 1 celery stalk (cut)

• 3 cloves of garlic
• 5 fresh shiitake mushrooms
• 120 ml of coconut oil
• 1 teaspoon sesame oi l
• 3 tbsp dashi granules
• 2 teaspoons of salt

Broth:
• 2 teaspoons unsalted butter (per serving)
• Low-sodium chicken or vegetable broth (235 ml per serving)
• Mirin (sweet rice wine; 2 teaspoons per portion)

• 1 large rectangular piece of kombu (approx. 25 cm long, roughly cut)
• Dried shiitake mushrooms (crushed; 2 mushrooms per serving)

Preparation:

1. Put the carrot, onion, spring onion, apple, garlic cloves and the fresh shiitake mushrooms in a food processor and chop everything until a paste is formed.

2. Heat the coconut oil and sesame oil in a medium saucepan over medium heat. Add the fruit and vegetable paste and cook for about 10-12 minutes. Then add the dashi granules and the salt. Stir well.

3. For the broth, put the butter in a large saucepan and set it on medium heat. When the butter begins to turn slightly brown and smell nutty, add the chicken or vegetable broth, mirin, kombu and dried shiitake mushrooms. Bring it to a boil. Then reduce the heat and let it simmer for 15 minutes. Use a slotted spoon to remove the coarser pieces. Add the Shio vegetable and fruit base (yes, 3 tsp serving). Put 235 ml each in a soup bowl. Add pasta and toppings as desired.

Simple & strong base broth

Preparation time: 1.5 hours, servings: 4

Nutritional information: calories: 12.8 kcal, carbohydrates: 2.3 g, fat: 0.12 g, protein: 0.54 g

Ingredients:

- 1 onion (peeled and roughly chopped)
- 1 carrot (peeled and roughly chopped)
- ½ stick of leek (roughly cut)
- 50 g ginger (sliced)
- 1 clove of garlic (peeled)
- 350 g pork ribs
- 1 small beef marrow bone
- 4 chicken wings
- 1 dried shiitake mushroom
- 1 tbsp dried sardines
- 5 g kombu
- 1 teaspoon pepper
- 1 teaspoon salt
- water

Preparation:

1. First, fry the onion. Then add all the other ingredients to the pot. Cover everything with water and let the soup simmer for about 4 hours.
2. Pour the broth off through a fine sieve. Add as much water as you have about 1.2 liters of broth.
3. Put 235 ml each in a soup bowl. Add pasta and toppings as desired.

Tonyu broth

Preparation time: 1 hour, servings: 4

Nutritional information: calories: 514 kcal, carbohydrates: 28.4 g, fat: 22.6 g, protein: 46.4 g

Ingredients:

- 500 g turkey bones (broken)
- 1 liter of soy milk
- 20 g ginger (sliced)
- 1 stick of leek (finely chopped)
- salt
- 400 ml of water

Preparation:

1. Take a large saucepan and add the turkey bones, leek, ginger and 400 ml of water.
2. Let everything cook for about 15 minutes with the lid closed.
3. Open the lid and wait until the broth has reduced to approx. 100-150 ml.
4. Add the soy milk and let it cook for another 10 minutes. Warning: soy milk burns easily.
4. Strain the broth. Put 235 ml each in a soup bowl. Add pasta and toppings as desired.

Tonkotsu broth

Preparation time: 8-10 hours, servings: 8

Nutritional information **:** calories: 593kcal, carbohydrates: 32g, fat: 36g, protein: 36g

Ingredients:

- 1.4 kg pork feet (sliced)
- 1 kg of chicken wings
- 500 g of bacon
- 1 onion (peeled and roughly chopped)
- 8 spring onions (roughly chopped)
- 1 head of garlic (peeled and roughly chopped)
- 20 g ginger (sliced)
- 200 g shiitake mushrooms (roughly chopped)
- 2 tablespoons of peppercorn s
- salt
- approx. 4 liters of water

Preparation:

1. First, wash pork feet and chicken wings carefully. Put them in a saucepan, cover everything with water and bring to a boil. Wait until the water bubbles up vigorously. Take the saucepan off the stove, pour off the water and let the parts cool down briefly.
2. Sear the onion, spring onions, garlic and ginger in a pan for about 15 minutes.
3. Put the blanched pork feet and chicken wings with the bacon, vegetables, shiitake mushrooms and peppercorns in a large saucepan and cover with approx. 4 liters of water.
4. Bring the water to a boil and regularly skim off the foam that forms.
5. After about half an hour, close the pot with a lid and let it simmer for 4 hours. Remove the bacon you will cook the broth for another 6 to 8 hours.
6. Finally, season the soup with salt and strain through a fine sieve.
7. Put 235 ml each in a soup bowl. Add pasta and toppings as desired.

Vegan dashi broth

Preparation time: 1 hour, servings: 4

Nutritional information: calories: 12.8 kcal, carbohydrates: 2.3 g, fat: 0.12 g, protein: 0.54 g

Ingredients:

- 25 g shiitake mushrooms (dried)
- 10 g kombu
- 1 liter of wate r

Preparation:

1. Take a pot with min. 500 ml capacity and put the Shiitake Pile in one pot and kombu in the other.
2. Bring both pots to a boil and then let them simmer for 1 hour.
3. Finally, strain off the ingredients and add the two brews together.
4. Put 235 ml each in a soup bowl. Add pasta and toppings as desired.

Vegetarian Kotteri broth

Preparation time: 2 hours, servings: 8

Nutritional information **:** calories: 752 kcal, carbohydrates: 72g, fat: 14 g, protein: 50 g

Ingredients:

- 500 g butternut squash (approx. 300 g peeled and roughly cut)
- 2 onions (peeled and roughly chopped)
- 3 cloves of garlic (peeled)
- 100 g of fresh shiitake mushrooms
- 6 dried shiitake mushrooms
- 6-8 g kombu
- 2 liters of water

- 2 teaspoons of paprika powder
- 2 tbsp ginger (chopped)
- 75 ml soy sauce
- 4 WL miso paste
- 3 tbsp rice vinegar
- 3 tbsp coconut oil
- 2 teaspoons of salt
- olive oi l

Preparation:

1. Preheat the oven to 250 ° C.
2. Take a large saucepan and bring about 2 liters of water to a boil. Add the dried shiitake mushrooms and kombu. Reduce the heat and let everything simmer for about 1 hour.
3. Mix the pumpkin, onions, garlic and the fresh shiitake mushrooms with a little olive oil and paprika and spread it on a baking sheet.
4. Cook the vegetables in the oven for about 15 minutes. Reduce the temperature to 225 ° C and cook for another 15 minutes.
5. After the broth has simmered for an hour, remove the mushrooms and kombu, and add the vegetables and ginger. Let the broth simmer for 20 minutes with the lid closed.
6. Puree the broth finely.
7. Then add miso paste, soy sauce, rice vinegar, coconut oil and salt and puree the broth again. If necessary, the broth can be diluted with water.
8. Put 235 ml each in a soup bowl. Add pasta and toppings as desired.

Umami vegetable broth

Preparation time: 3 hours, servings: 12

Nutritional information: calories: 991 kcal, carbohydrates: 115 g, fat: 30.5 g, protein: 37.7 g

Ingredients:

- 2 tbsp light miso paste
- 2 tbsp rapeseed oil
- 2 tablespoons of wate r
- 2 onions (peeled and finely chopped)
- 2 carrots (peeled and finely chopped)
- 4 celery stalks (finely chopped)
- 1 stick of leek (finely chopped)

- 1 bulb of fennel (finely chopped)
- 5 coriander roots
- 1 head of garlic (halved)
- ½ bunch of flat-leaf parsley
- 5 dried shiitake mushrooms
- 20 g kombu
- 2 teaspoons of salt

- 1 teaspoon black pepper
- 2 bay leaves
- ½ teaspoon yellow mustard seeds
- ½ teaspoon coriander seeds
- 3.5 liters of water

Preparation:

1. Mix the miso paste with the rapeseed oil and 2 tablespoons of water and set aside.
2. Place the vegetables, kombu and shiitake mushrooms on a baking sheet. Drizzle the mixed miso paste over it. Leave the whole thing in the oven for 1 hour at 150 ° C. Turn it over in between.
3. Then put the roasted vegetables in a large saucepan. Add the spices and pour in water. Bring everything to a boil, reduce the heat and then let it simmer for 1.5 hours.
4. Put 235 ml each in a soup bowl. Add pasta and toppings as desired.

Miso soy broth

Preparation time: 1 hour, servings: 2

Nutritional information: calories: 245 kcal, carbohydrates: 23.1 g, fat: 10 g, protein: 13.2 g

Ingredients:

- 1 onion (peeled and finely chopped)
- 1 heaped teaspoon ginger (finely chopped)
- 12 g miso paste
- 0.5 l of water
- 0.5 l of soy milk

Preparation:

1. Firstly, fry the ginger and onion.
2. Add the miso paste and fry it briefly.
3. Add water and soy milk and let everything simmer for at least half an hour.
4. Put 235 ml each in a soup bowl. Add pasta and toppings as desired.

Assari broth (mushroom broth)

Preparation time: 4 hours, servings: 8

Nutritional information: calories: 441 kcal, carbohydrates: 58 g, fat: 5 g, protein: 27 g

Ingredients:

- 300 g fresh shitake mushrooms
- 12 dried shiitake mushrooms
- 6 dried morels
- 12 g kombu
- 20 g ginger (sliced)
- 2 spring onions
- 150 ml soy sauce
- 2.5 liters of water

Preparation:

1. Put the shiitake mushrooms, kombu, ginger and spring onions in a large saucepan.

2.   Pour everything up with 2.5 liters of water, add the soy sauce and let it simmer for 30 minutes

3.   Remove the mushroom broth from the heat and let it steep for at least 3 hours. Then strain the soup.

4.   Put 235 ml each in a soup bowl. Add pasta and toppings as desired.

Niboshi Dashi

Preparation time: 1 hour + 1 day, servings: 8

Nutritional information **:** calories: 193.6 kcal, carbohydrates: 11.8 g, fat: 3.3 g, protein: 29.4 g

Ingredients:

- 625 ml of water
- 90 g Niboshi (dried anchovies)
- Kombu (2.5-7.5 cm)
- 15 g bonito flakes

Preparation:

1.   Put the water, niboshi and kombu together in a saucepan and leave in the refrigerator overnight.

2.   Bring the mixture to a boil, then remove the kombu. Let it simmer for another 40 minutes.

3.   Add the bonito flakes and simmer for another 10 minutes.

4.   Strain the broth.

Ramen noodles

Preparation time: 2 ½ hours, servings: 4

Nutritional information: calories: 770 kcal, carbohydrates: 164 g, fat: 2 g, protein: 20.1 g

Ingredients:

- 1 packet of baking powder
- 100 ml of water
- 200 g of flour
- 1 pinch of salt
- Corn starch for dusting

Preparation:

1.   Preheat the oven to 130 ° C. Sprinkle the baking powder on a baking sheet lined with baking paper and bake for about 1 hour. Then fill it into a well-sealable container.

2.   Take 2 level teaspoons of the baked baking powder and stir it into the water. Put the flour in a bowl and add salt and water.

3.   Knead everything until a crumbly dough is formed. Turn the dough out onto a clean work surface and knead it by hand for about 5 minutes. Wrap the dough in cling film and let it rest for about 15 minutes at room temperature.

4.   Knead the dough again for about 5 minutes (roll out and fold up). The dough should only have a few cracks. Wrap the dough in cling film and let it rest for another hour.

5.   Divide the dough into four portions and gradually roll it out to approx. 1 mm with a pasta machine. Then twist it through the spaghetti attachment. Shape the noodles into nests in portions and sprinkle with the cornstarch. Boil the pasta in salted water for about 1 minute until firm to the bite.

Tonkotsu Ramen with Chashu and Ajitsuke Tamago

Preparation time: 30 minutes, servings: 4

Nutritional information: calories: 7006 kcal, carbohydrates: 864 g, fat: 244 g, protein: 355 g

Ingredients:

- 60 ml Shio broth
- 1 liter of Tonkotsu broth
- 1 teaspoon soy sauce
- Pinch of salt
- 1 teaspoon coconut oil
- 12 pieces of Chashu (see page 122)

- 4 servings of ramen noodles
- 2 Ajitsuke Tamago (see page 124)
- 1 spring onion (sliced)
- 30 g Beni Shoga (see page 123)
- Mayu (see page 126)

Preparation:

1.   Put two spoons of the Shio broth in each soup bowl.

2.   Heat the Tonkotsu broth in a large saucepan. Add the soy sauce and salt.

3.   Sear the chashu in a pan for 1-2 minutes on each side.

4.   Cook the ramen noodles.

5.   Put the finished noodles in the soup bowl and add about 250 ml Tonkotsu broth to each bowl. Add 3 pieces of chashu, ½ ajitsuke tamago, spring onions, 1 teaspoon Beni Shoga and ½ teaspoon mayu to each bowl.